TASTING WINE & CHEESE

TASTING WINE & CHEESE

AN INSIDER'S GUIDE TO MASTERING THE PRINCIPLES OF PAIRING

ADAM CENTAMORE

Quarry Books
100 Cummings Center, Suite 406L
Beverly, MA 01915

quarrybooks.com • quarryspoon.com

Quarto is the authority on a wide range of topics.

Quarto educates, entertains and enriches the lives of our readers—enthusiasts and lovers of hands-on living.

www.quartoknows.com

10 9 8 7 6 5 4 3 2 1

ISBN: 978-1-63159-067-2

Digital edition published in 2015
eISBN: 978-1-62788-727-4

Library of Congress Cataloging-in-Publication Data available.

Design: Emily Portnoi
Page layout: *tabula rasa* graphic design
Cover image: Glenn Scott Photography
Photography: Glenn Scott Photography, except pages 35, 49, 53, 57, 73, 74, 100, 112, 142, 144, 145, 146, 147 Shutterstock

Printed in China

For those who love to eat, drink, and learn.

CONTENTS

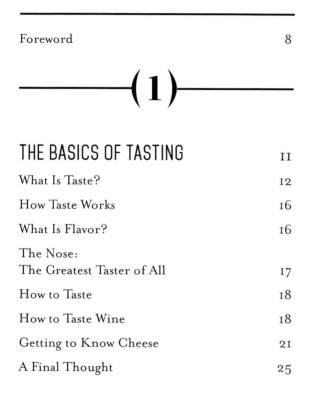

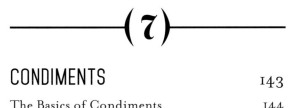

(5)

RED WINES 87

(6)

DESSERT AND FORTIFIED WINES 127

(7)

CONDIMENTS 143

FOREWORD

The sensual pleasures are the magic of life. Our visual senses are fulfilled marveling at Caravaggio's Conversion of Saint Paul; *our auditory senses through music such as* An Alpine Symphony *by Richard Strauss; our skin and our touch revealing to us softness and texture; and of course, smells through our nose and tastes through our lips and tongue. These are all pathways to make our hearts smile.*

As always in life, one does not know what one does not know. However, when one has a framework and a context, things connect with each other. This leads to an understanding of our experiences that not only gives us fulfillment and satisfaction, but a sense of empowerment. Perhaps E.E. Cummings said it best when he said: "Hell is a place where nothing connects with nothing." In contrast, a deeper understanding of phenomena and experiences where things connect, simply stated, is the joy of learning.

Adam Centamore has written an excellent primer on the pairing of wine and cheese. This is a subject that is Adam's passion, and one he has studied and mastered. This is a book that will give the reader a framework, enabling one to navigate through countless pairing possibilities and be able to express the nuances of pairing wine and cheese. It is a marvelous book written in a style that is endearing and easy to follow. Adam's goal throughout the book is to teach us the basics so that we can continue to learn for the rest of our lives. This perhaps is the best gift any author can bestow on his or her readers.

I first met Adam at the Confrérie de Bourgogne Chevaliers du Tastevin membership committee dinner when he was presented to us as a potential candidate. This was a meeting of the officers and potential candidates. When Adam had the floor, and shared with us what he does and how he developed his passion, it became abundantly clear to us we had a solid new member of the order. He was then elevated to Maitre d'Fromage in the Sous-Commanderie de Boston, and has been an asset to our organization ever since.

The nucleation point for this book occurred at the Worcester Art Museum in Massachusetts, where we held an event comparing French cheeses and U.S. artisanal cheeses along with pairing Burgundian wines. Adam was the host and organized the tasting. All of this was done in a blind tasting mode, in which participants did not know whether the cheeses were French or domestic. The participants were members of the Chevaliers du Tastevin as well as some members of the International Wine and Food Society of Boston; a group that has a good palate and is well heeled in the culinary arts. Much to our surprise, the participants did not do well in the blind tasting and only 3 or 4 persons (out of 45) called it right. This says much about artisanal cheeses from Vermont and other parts of the United States, and also to Adam's "trickeries" of selecting the contestant cheeses!

During the tasting, Adam presented a tutorial with each flight and course, and it was one of the most lucid, compelling, and interesting set of mini-lectures I had heard. The professor in me saw another professor and a great teacher at work. At the break, I approached Adam and did not suggest, but rather boldly told him, that he has to write a book on wine and cheese pairing, because there is a need for such a book. More importantly, the experience we just had at the tasting is one that needs to be experienced by as many others as possible. I still recall Adam's face when I suggested that he write a book. He looked at me and I am sure to this day that he wondered whether I had more wine than cheese and whether I was serious. Needless to say, the idea of such a book was reinforced in Adam, and over a period of a few months, he was nudged as to how the book was coming along. Encouragement by friends and loved ones is a huge catalyst to get us to do the things that we do. Adam has certainly risen to the occasion, and this book, which you are about to immerse yourself in, will be a joyous experience.

I want to take this opportunity to thank Adam for archiving and documenting this wonderful book, which I hope will be the first of many more to come.

Diran Apelian
Alcoa-Howmet Professor of Engineering (WPI)
Grand Sénechal Emerité (2009 to 2014),
Chevaliers du Tastevin (Boston)
President, International Wine and Food Society
(Boston), 2014 to present

(1)

THE BASICS OF TASTING

What does wine taste like? How about cheese? What does anything taste like? It sounds like such a simple question, but it can be tricky to answer. Every time a bite of food is taken or a drink sipped, tastes and flavors are released. But how much attention do we pay beyond what we need to form a basic judgment of whether or not it "tastes good"? We come equipped with a phenomenally sophisticated array of sensory equipment, which is fortunate, because wine and cheese are incredibly complex foods. It's important to understand how to get the most enjoyment out of them.

The human senses of smell and taste are inextricably linked. Without one, the other is dull and uninteresting when we are eating and drinking. Together, they provide symphonies of flavor and waves of sensory pleasure. Despite such magnificent and complex abilities, not many people consider the basics of taste and how their senses play a vital role in getting the most from their food and wine experience. This chapter talks about how taste works, how to taste wine and cheese, and why it matters.

Humans perceive five tastes: sweet, salty, bitter, sour, and umami.

WHAT IS TASTE?

Taste is a chemical sensory impression taken by your tongue when eating or drinking, and is one of five generally recognized senses (along with hearing, touch, sight, and smell). Humans perceive five basic tastes: sweet, salty, bitter, sour, and umami.

SWEET

Sweet is found in simple carbohydrates, especially sugar. It is generally regarded as the most pleasurable of the five tastes. This is thought to have been evolutionarily advantageous because sweet foods (and carbohydrates in general) are extremely energy dense, a valuable trait for early humans trying to consume and store energy when food was scarce.

SALTY

Salty is a taste triggered by the presence of sodium ions on the tongue (table salt, for example, is made of sodium chloride). Salty is another pleasurable taste, although the threshold for being "too much," and consequently unpleasant, is far lower than sweet is for most people. Ever had popcorn with too much salt on it? Yuck.

Dark chocolate is bitter, while unsweetened tea is astringent.

BITTER

This taste is often confused with astringent. Bitter is a taste that is sharp and unpleasant. Biting into an orange to start peeling it, for example, releases the bitter oil under the rind. Bitterness is also found in plain black coffee and unsweetened dark chocolate. Astringency is a physically drying, puckering sensation, not a taste. Walnut skins and freshly brewed, unsweetened tea are astringent. They leave the mouth feeling dry and sandpapery. Bitterness is the most sensitive and unpleasant of the tastes, which is good because many toxic compounds found in nature taste bitter, and are therefore less likely to be eaten!

BITTER VERSUS ASTRINGENT

Bitter and astringent are often confused. Bitter is a flavor, best recognized as the sharp taste found in the skins of citrus fruits or in dark chocolate. Ever bite into an orange peel? That's bitterness. Astringency is a tactile feeling in your mouth. The clearest example of astringency is found in freshly brewed tea. Before adding cream or sugar, take a sip of the tea. Feel your mouth dry out? The tannins in the tea leave your mouth with a sandpapery texture—astringency.

SOUR

Sour is the taste that conveys the amount of acidity in foods, and is most commonly sensed by the edges of the tongue. Foods that have a balanced amount of acidity taste lively and refreshing, especially wine. Too much acidity, though, and that same food or wine tastes sour. Sweet and sour work together closely in foods, particularly fruit. At a strawberry's peak of ripeness, for example, the sweet and acidic characteristics are balanced, and that delicious strawberry is at once bright and tangy, and pleasantly sweet. As the fruit continues to ripen past its peak, the acidity lessens and the flavor becomes less appealing because that balance is no longer there. Fresh lemon juice is a great example of sourness.

UMAMI

A word meaning "delicious taste" in Japanese, umami is a savory taste that some people also describe as "meaty" or "brothy." Umami comes from the presence of glutamic acid, which is an amino acid. The strongest taste of umami can be found in soy sauce. Mushrooms, tomatoes, and some fermented foods also have umami taste. Monosodium glutamate (MSG), a flavor enhancer often used in cooking, adds umami taste to foods. Because umami is sensed through the mouth's glutamate glands (and not as a result of the presence of sodium ions, as salty is), food scientists generally regard it as a separate taste from saltiness.

This list is what modern Western science considers basic or fundamental tastes. Some cultures may consider other tastes to be fundamental as well, viewing these five tastes as an incomplete list. For example, many Asian cultures historically consider spiciness or pungency (particularly from chile peppers) to be additional tastes. Even the list of five tastes we accept now was only four prior to the early twentieth century (umami wasn't added to the list until 1908). Food scientists and biologists are always looking to refine and sharpen our understanding of how we interpret tastes.

TRY IT!

Getting to Know the Five Tastes. Set out a spoonful of sugar (sweet), a pinch of salt (salty), a wedge of fresh lemon (sour), a cup of freshly brewed black coffee (bitter), and a sip of soy sauce (umami). Try each of them side by side to see how different they are. For many people, this simple demonstration clarifies each taste, especially similar sensations like bitter and sour.

Get to know the tastes: sugar (sweet), lemon (sour), salt (salty), coffee beans (bitter), soy sauce (umami).

HOW TASTE WORKS

The human tongue is covered with thousands of papillae (hairlike structures that give your tongue its rough texture). Most of these papillae each contain hundreds of taste buds, located on the front and back of the tongue. The roof and sides of the mouth contain taste buds as well, but in lower quantities.

Each of these buds contains receptor cells dedicated to taste. When a food or beverage is chewed or sipped, molecules are released in the mouth and land on these taste buds. Different molecular compositions trigger different responses in each receptor. For example, when hydrogen ions are released from a piece of sour candy, taste bud receptors sense these particular ions, sending the information to the brain, which then identifies the taste as "sour." Each of the other tastes has its own triggers that help the brain recognize individual tastes.

Remember, though, that the taste of a food or beverage is only part of what the brain uses to form an impression of it. Many other factors are subconsciously considered while coming up with a final evaluation. Temperature, texture, aroma, and other factors work together with taste to form a composite impression. This is where flavor comes into the picture.

WHAT IS FLAVOR?

Taste is a singular, particular sensory impression. It can't convey a complete description of what you're eating or drinking. It can, however, convey an aspect of it.

For example, saying pizza tastes salty is accurate. Or, saying the root beer you're having with it tastes sweet is also spot-on. For many people, when they say "taste," they actually mean "flavor."

Flavor is the total impression of something consumed. Flavor considers all aspects of the food or drink. That includes the temperature of the pizza, the saltiness of the cheese, the texture of the crust, and the piquancy of the roasted jalapeño peppers (did I mention the roasted jalapeños? They are just fabulous on pepperoni pizza). Of all these different aspects, the perception of flavor relies most heavily on the taste and aroma of what is being eaten. It is through these two senses that the most information is gathered for the brain to come to a conclusion. This is where the nose contributes, and plays a tremendously important role.

TASTE VERSUS FLAVOR

Imagine sitting down to enjoy a meal—perhaps a slice or two of pepperoni pizza. The slices are still hot, and the aromas of melted mozzarella cheese and spicy salami waft up to greet you. You take a bite and chew it, savoring the richness of the meat, the saltiness of the cheese, the buttery and crispy crust. With a smile you think, "This tastes delicious." Sorry to say, but you've just made one of the most common mistakes in describing food!

THE NOSE: THE GREATEST TASTER OF ALL

When I make that statement in my classes, I usually get at least a few quizzical looks. I completely understand why. After all, the nose is for smelling and the tongue is for tasting, right?

On the surface, it seems so. However, the reality is much more complex. Your nose and sense of smell play a critical part in how flavors are interpreted in foods and beverages, especially wine and cheese. Believe it or not, you already sort of know this. And I can prove it.

Think of the last time you had a stuffed-up nose from a cold. Someone takes pity on you and makes you a bowl of chicken noodle soup. You're lying in bed watching a bad movie marathon, and your friend brings it in. From across the room, you see the steam rising up from the bowl. You can already taste the garlicky broth, the saltiness from the grated pecorino cheese, and the peppery bite from the dried pepperoncini (I'm Sicilian, so crushed red pepper and pecorino cheese go on almost everything). Your mouth waters as you pick up the spoon, fully anticipating deliciousness. You scoop a big spoonful into your mouth and . . . taste practically nothing. Maybe there's a slight hint of garlic or saltiness, but otherwise it's just a bowl of bland, hot liquid filled with even blander foods. So disappointing. What happened? The good news is your tongue isn't broken. The bad news? Your nose isn't in the game, and it took flavor with it.

When you like (or dislike) the flavor of something, a majority of that perception is based on the aroma of what was consumed. Even if it doesn't seem like you smelled what was being eaten, aromatic molecules still added lots of information as you chewed.

When you bring something to your nose to smell it, you inhale. That action creates an air current, pulling molecules from the item being smelled. Those molecules are channeled into the nose, collected in the nasal cavity in the back, and focused onto the olfactory epithelium (specialized tissue designed only for smelling). Special detectors called chemoreceptors sense airborne aromatic molecules and pass coded electrical information on to the brain. Patterns in electrical information are recognized, and a smell is perceived.

Some research suggests that, unlike the receptors the tongue uses to detect taste, the chemoreceptors in the nasal cavity are highly specialized. This suggests every receptor on the surface of the olfactory epithelium is designed to be sensitive to a particular family of related molecules, and may be more sensitive to some than others, helping to differentiate between aromas more effectively.

Temperature and relative humidity also have an effect on the intensity of an aroma. That's why cold foods don't really smell like much—the lower temperature means less molecular movement and therefore less information for the nose to pick up on. The converse is true for hot foods—higher temperature means greater molecular activity and an easier time picking up the information. The molecule's solubility is also a factor. Molecules that dissolve more easily in water tend to be stronger, and therefore easier to detect.

All these elements work together to provide the mouth and brain the information it needs to make decisions and recognize preferences. When it all happens, it can be a tidal wave of information. It may seem a little daunting to try and tackle it all at once. What is the best way to receive all this information? What is the most efficient way to make sense of everything being experienced? What should one be looking for? What is important? What is the process?

In short, how does one taste?

HOW TO TASTE

If you have ever read a book on tasting wine or cheese, or taken a class in appreciating these foods, the author or teacher most likely presented his or her preferred system for tasting, that is, the procedure for tasting he or she feels is most effective. It may at first seem a bit of a buzzkill to evaluate a new cheese or wine with a critical eye. After all, isn't part of the fun the romance of a morsel of cheese with a chunk of freshly made baguette and a sip of satisfying wine? Shouldn't serendipity reign? Damn the torpedoes and full cheese ahead?

The idea behind a consistent, progressive tasting method is not to take the fun out of eating or drinking. Quite the opposite! By paying closer attention to the characteristics of what is being consumed, *really* paying attention, the most pleasure and understanding possible are extracted. The goal of a tasting system is consistency—doing it each time you eat cheese or sip wine. Fortunately, the more it is done, the easier and more automatic it becomes. I can promise this—if done consistently for a while, it will become so automatic that you will hardly even notice it. The payoff, getting the most pleasure from wine and cheese, is gratifying and well worth the effort.

HOW TO TASTE WINE

Wine is marvelously complex. Along with coffee, wine is by far the most complex liquid we drink. With each sip, hundreds of compounds are released, each providing flavors and aromas to consider.

Some are common and familiar—strawberry, lemon, or cherry, for example. Some are a bit more esoteric (when was the last time a wine smelled like wet graphite, or had the flavor of boysenberry to you?). Our task as nerds and enthusiasts is to extract the most information we can, in the best way possible. When evaluating a wine or cheese beyond the simple "I like it," we care about three basic characteristics: what it looks like, what it smells like, and what it tastes like.

THE LOOK

Take a peek at the glass of wine you're enjoying. Much information can be garnered just by looking.

What color is the wine? Simple, right? It's red. Or it's white. Or pink. Those are pretty much the three basic wine colors, but we can do better than that. Take it a step further. What kind of red is it? Bricks are a different red than garnet, for example. In white wines, canary yellow is far different than a bar of gold. For rosé wines, light salmon-colored pink is more delicate than strawberry pink, a much darker color. Consider how light catching or "alive" the wine looks. Is the color vibrant and crisp, or is it tired looking and dull? For the best results, examine wine held against a white background such as a sheet of paper or a tablecloth. It's amazing how much the color of the background can change the color of the wine.

Tilt your glass 45 degrees to see the difference between the edge and the center of the wine.

Tilt the glass to a 45-degree angle (be careful not to spill). Look at the edge where the wine meets the glass, called the rim. Wine nerds compare that to the center of the wine in the glass, called the core. That rim-to-core variation is important because it gives us clues regarding the wine's age and how it was made. For example, deeper shades of yellow in a white wine suggest aging. In some red wines, hints of blue at the rim suggest lower acidity.

THE SMELL

This is really where most of the evaluating takes place. Tasting is important, of course, but the nose is doing most of the heavy lifting and so plays a leading role in making evaluations.

Set the glass down and allow the wine to come to a rest. Put your nose in the glass a bit and take a deep whiff. Really inhale (the deeper the inhale, the more molecules make it into the nose). What does it smell like? (Don't worry if all you come up with is "wine." When starting, that's common. It gets better, and quickly.) Does it smell like flowers? Fruit? Herbs? Try to be as specific as possible. Are there aromas of fruit? If so, is it light fruit (apples, nectarines, citrus) or dark fruit (blackberry, cherry, strawberry)? You're at a bit of a disadvantage here because all there is to consider is the smell, nothing else. When holding a lemon, visual and tactile clues confirm what the nose is reporting. When considering a glass of wine, those are removed from the picture, making it harder to pick out and identify just the aromas. As with anything else, practice makes perfect. The more attention paid to the aromas of food each time you eat, the easier it becomes to recall them later.

Now gently swirl the glass (either on the tabletop or in your hand). Take another deep whiff. Notice anything different? Absolutely! Every aroma seems easier to detect. The action of swirling the wine agitates it a bit, allowing oxygen to blend in and release more molecules to be sensed.

THE FLAVOR

Tasting wine is a great way not only to enjoy it, but also to get to know it. It's usually the reason we have the glass in the first place, right?

Take a small sip of the wine and let it sit on the tongue. Don't swallow it. After a few seconds, your mouth will warm the wine, making it easier to perceive. Gently swish it around, letting it touch every surface of your mouth. Then, spit it out or swallow it (if swallowing, the senses begin to dull a bit from the alcohol. For non-nerds, this is often the whole point!). Notice which tastes are revealed. Is it tart? Bitter? Sweet? Does it have flavors of limes or mangoes? Does your mouth feel dry and puckery after swallowing?

Take a second sip and employ the "slurp" technique to aerate the wine (mix it with oxygen). It may seem a bit awkward at first, but a little practice will quickly help. Take a small sip and let it sit on the tongue. Now pretend the wine is super-hot soup that needs to be cooled, and spitting it out isn't an option. Purse your lips and quickly inhale, forcing air over the surface of the wine. In this case, you're not concerned with the temperature of the wine (as you would be with scalding-hot soup). For wine, forcing air over it agitates it and "wakes it up," in the same way swirling your glass woke up the aromas. Doing this "slurp" doesn't add any flavor information. Rather, it turns up the volume of what is already there, making it easier for you to perceive.

After swallowing (or spitting out) the wine, pay attention to how the wine makes your mouth feel. Does it leave it dry? Refreshed or dulled? Pay attention to how long you can taste the wine after it is gone. That persistence of flavor perception is called the finish of a wine. The longer your perception of the flavor remains, the longer the finish.

GETTING TO KNOW CHEESE

In many ways, you taste and evaluate cheese the same way you do wine. You pay attention to the look, smell, and flavors of the cheese. When thinking about cheese, however, a different set of adjectives is usually used (I don't know whether I'd ever want to come across a wine I found to be "pleasantly moldy"). Texture is also an important consideration because there is such a broad variety.

THE LOOK

Cheese can be quite beautiful to look it. From the pure, bright white of fresh goat cheese to the mottled and complex interior of blue cheese, every cheese tells a story through its appearance.

Take a moment to look closely at the cheese. Examine the colors of both the exterior (the rind) and the interior (the paste). Are the colors consistent and even over the entire surface, or do some areas have different coloration than others? Look at the texture of the rind—are there any bumps or cracks? Is the rind even over the whole wheel, or is it drier in some places? After cutting a slice, compare the center of the wedge to the cheese just underneath the rind. Because cheese develops from the outside in, you will most likely see a difference.

In a slice of Bûcheron, it's easy to see the differences from the rind to the center.

Blue cheese aromas are usually easier to detect than those of other cheeses.

THE SMELL

Wine comes from fruit, and cheese comes from milk. That difference alone guarantees a different set of adjectives will come into play, right? What may be surprising, however, are the similarities in aroma that you may discover. It's not unusual for both to display aromas that are lactic, or earthy, or grassy. They can have different expressions of these smells, but they may be closer than you'd expect.

When smelling a piece of cheese, get a good whiff. With some cheeses, that won't be a problem whatsoever (certain washed-rind and blue cheeses will be noticeable the moment they are brought into the room). Whether it means bringing the cheese right up to your nose, or maintaining a respectable distance, take note of what you smell. Where wines can smell like cherries, lemons, or vanilla, cheeses can smell animally, or yeasty, or moldy (a great trait in some cheeses, not so much in wines). Does the cheese smell grassy, or woodsy? Can you smell the animal's raw milk? For example, many sheep milk cheeses retain the farmy, animal smell of the ewe. The aroma may be mild or it may be prominent, but it's pretty much always there. Does the cheese smell pleasant or off-putting? Taking note of these kinds of characteristics adds another layer of information for you to consider as you get to know the cheese and, ultimately, form an opinion.

THE SMELL OF FEAR

No other food can confuse and intimidate people with just a smell quite like cheese can. For some, the aggressive and pungent aromas of a washed-rind cheese are heavenly; for others, they are almost unbearable. Some cheeses are so mildly aromatic that they have to be inches from your nose to even sense them. There are cheeses that smell like powerhouses, yet are mild and creamy on the inside. Others are gentle on the nose and chainsaws on the tongue. With cheese, the good news regarding aroma can also be the bad news—few cheeses taste anything like they smell! The classic French cheese Époisses may smell like a sucker punch, but the interior is nothing but sweet, milky hugs. When getting to know a piece of cheese, absolutely smell it. Just keep in mind that the aroma is only one part of the overall picture.

THE FEEL

The texture of cheese plays an important part in your evaluation of it. In wines, texture is important, but usually has less of an impact on your impression. Wines tend to have similar textures based on their type—dessert wines are typically thicker and more viscous than other wines, for example, but most dessert wines will give you the same general impression. With cheeses, those textural variations can be greater and more intense, even within the same style of cheese.

Cheeses can have a wide range of textures.

Without feeling too self-conscious, take a small crumb of the cheese you're considering and rub it between your fingers. Notice how easily (or not) it smears. A cheese with lots of moisture, such as Brie, will smear quite easily, whereas a drier, firmer cheese such as Parmigiano-Reggiano will simply crumble into smaller pieces.

Take a small bite, and let it sit on your tongue for a moment. Notice how firm or soft the cheese feels. As it warms, it will soften a little more. Now slowly chew it, paying attention to the physical impression the cheese makes. Is it soft and pliable, or is it a hard cheese that becomes a little granular as you chew?

TIME, TEMPERATURE, AND TENDERNESS

Cheese, like most foods, will reveal the most information when at room temperature. If the cheese is too cold, the aromatic compounds are stiff and muted, and the cheese won't smell like much. Too hot, and the cheese's aromas will become cloying and unpleasant (not to mention the cheese will probably ooze a bit). Ideally, cheese is best examined, and served, after an hour or so out of the fridge. That time allows the cheese to gently come up to room temperature, making it at its best for smelling and, most important, eating!

THE FLAVOR

Now we come to the main attraction. As with wine, people usually have a piece of cheese to eat it, not simply to contemplate it! Soon enough, you'll be eating the cheese for the sheer pleasure of it, but first spend a minute appreciating the tastes and flavors of cheese.

When tasting cheese for the first time, less is more. Take a small bite—the smaller amount will be easier to manipulate in the mouth. Let it rest in your mouth for ten seconds or so. That is enough time for the cheese to warm a bit and release more information, making it easier to sense. What do you taste? Maybe the saltiness is prominent, or maybe the cheese has a peppery bite. Is it bitter? Metallic? Sweet? Cheese can display an amazing range of tastes and flavors. The more attention you pay, the more the cheese will tell you.

Like most nerds, I do NOT employ these techniques with every cheese and wine I encounter! I enjoy a plain ol' wedge of pepper Jack cheese or sip of cheap-o Pinot Grigio as much as anyone else. I do, however, use these techniques whenever I encounter a new cheese or wine, or a new version or vintage of it. I use a great application on my tablet to keep track of my notes, making it a simple and effective way to remember what I have enjoyed. It only takes a few minutes, and I have the experience and my notes to draw from in the future. Then I nosh and gulp like everyone else!

A FINAL THOUGHT

The ability to taste food and appreciate flavors plays a significant and critical part in how much you enjoy (or don't) what you are eating and drinking. But it's not the whole picture.

Enjoying a particular taste or flavor is a little like reading individual words in a book. By themselves, the words may be funny or pleasing, but when they work together in sentences, true enjoyment comes. For pairing wine and cheese, the same idea applies. Tastes and flavors are fun to experience singly, but become something special when brought together in delicious ways. The total can be so much more than the sum of the parts! The next chapter talks about the fundamentals of doing just that.

(2)

THE BASICS OF PAIRING

Which wine goes best with fried chicken? How about blackened tuna steaks? Does red or white wine go better with cheese? What was once a simple mantra—red with meat, white with chicken and fish—is no longer all that simple. The culinary world is a much more expansive place than it once was, and people have access to more ingredients, techniques, and recipes than ever before. The relationship between wine and food is as important as ever, especially when that food is cheese. A fundamental understanding of pairing concepts is paramount. It's time to talk basics.

For many people, the thought of pairing a wine and a cheese is a little intimidating. Usually, it's because there are so many wines and cheeses from which to choose, and it can feel like the odds of making the "right" choice are very small. In reality, pairing food and drink isn't quite the monumental task it may seem. Once you understand a few basic principles, the possibilities are almost endless, especially with so many worldly ingredients available to the modern food enthusiast!

HOW TO THINK ABOUT PAIRING

Fundamentally, pairing is the art of bringing two or more ingredients together to create an outcome greater than the sum of the parts. Whether the ingredients are sandwiches and soda, chocolate and wine, or Scotch and cheese, the idea is the same. When professionals create a pairing, they consider the ingredients involved and their characteristics. What do they add to the combination? These characteristics can be anything, such as a particular temperature, an unusual texture, or a dominant flavor. Maybe it's the spicy bite of roasted jalapeño chiles, or the sweet viscosity of acacia honey, or the addition of a hot gravy or sauce. Whatever the contribution, a well-made pairing incorporates it to add to the overall experience.

When thinking about pairing, keep the end result in mind, even though the path to get there may seem a bit strange at times. Much of the fun comes from trying new and unusual ingredients together. When considering ingredients, don't dismiss something simply because it seems a little out of place. Although not every combination will work, great combinations can come from anywhere.

Odd combinations can be delicious.

Strange (but Tasty) Dishfellows. Rewarding pairings can come from the unlikeliest combinations. Try this: thinly slice a banana lengthwise. Top it with a few chopped walnuts, a pinch of minced parsley, and a small chunk of Parmigiano-Reggiano cheese. As odd as that sounds, it tastes pretty darn good. That combination is successful because all those foods have a similar density and weight in your mouth, and have flavor characteristics that work well together. It takes about the same amount of effort to chew walnuts as it does a piece of Parmigiano-Reggiano cheese, which makes it pleasant to chew together. The salty cheese is balanced by the sweetness of the banana. The parsley adds a fresh note to everything.

If you didn't try this experiment, not to worry. You've already had some of these ingredients together. Ever had a banana split? Bananas and walnuts. How about pesto? That probably included parsley, walnuts, and Parmigiano-Reggiano.

WHY PAIRING MATTERS

Why pair at all? I am asked that question surprisingly often. Virtually everything we eat and drink is consumed within the context of a pairing of some sort. Spaghetti and meatballs, peanut butter and jelly, and even salt and pepper are all pairings of sorts. For drinks, we mix all the time. Margaritas, strawberry milkshakes, and minty ice tea are all examples of pairings.

We even know what to avoid in an almost instinctual way. Have you ever seen anyone mix Worcestershire sauce into a tall, cold glass of milk? Of course not! Why? It's terrible. It even sounds terrible, doesn't it? There is a reason why trout-flavored gum doesn't exist. Some combinations just don't work well together.

Pairing food and drink matters because people enjoy eating and drinking and want to get the most enjoyment from it. We don't consume simply to continue existing. Cuisine, from the greatest Parisian restaurants to the simple and amazing street foods found in the smallest Mexican villages, exists because we care about it. Great pairings add to that enjoyment.

WHY MOST PEOPLE DON'T DO IT

People who are reluctant to explore pairings are usually so because they are afraid to fail, or it seems just too big a challenge, or maybe they have just never thought about it. All of these arguments are reasonable. Modern society's fascination (almost obsession) with food, wine, and cooking in general has resulted in a slew of expert personalities, cable programs, cookbooks, and myriad other avenues meant to generate awareness and profit for the industry. What was once something done without a thought by almost every mom on the planet is now the focus of adult education classes, college degree programs, and dictionary-sized how-to books. All that attention may make someone feel self-conscious or even unconfident in his or her tastes or abilities.

CHANGE THE PARADIGM!

Julia Child said it best: "The only real stumbling block is fear of failure. In cooking you've got to have a what-the-hell attitude." She may not have been speaking specifically of wine and cheese, but it certainly applies. The next time you have a piece of cheese or a glass of wine, consider the possibilities. There are lots of ways to enhance the pleasure of what you're about to eat or drink. Don't be afraid to think outside the rind: quite often you'll be rewarded. With wine and cheese pairing, one plus one doesn't equal two: it equals delicious.

GENERAL GUIDELINES FOR PAIRING

Pairing food and drink is, at the same time, amazingly easy and unbelievably hard. It's easy because we do it all the time, whether we are conscious of it or not. We employ combinations (and avoid most pitfalls) in our lives without giving it a second thought, and that is the hard part: creating great combinations, and doing so intentionally. For most, creating a wine and cheese pairing from scratch takes them out of their comfort zone, and that's where things start to get sketchy.

At its most basic, pairing is bringing two or more ingredients together in a way that creates an impression that is grander than the ingredients alone provide. It's that simple. Add lime juice to tequila? You've got yourself a pairing. Add barbecue sauce to grilled chicken—it's a pairing. Grate some Pecorino Romano over popcorn? Yep. That's a pairing. In each of these cases, the combination is more enjoyable than each ingredient alone might be. The secret to creating strong pairings is to consider each ingredient and how it contributes to the whole.

CONSIDER EACH INGREDIENT

Second-century Roman emperor Marcus Aurelius wrote, "Of each particular thing ask: what is it in itself? What is its nature?" I have to believe he enjoyed fantastic pairings when he ate and drank! When considering wine and cheese, that is the perfect question to ask. There are many ways foods and beverages express characteristics. The more clearly you can identify them, the better the pairing. Here are some significant characteristics to consider.

Dominant Flavors: Foods and wines usually have a dominant flavor. Strawberries have a dominant flavor of . . . strawberry. When ingredients are mixed together, it can be more challenging. What is the dominant flavor of a fruit salad? In that case, see whether one or two flavors speak more loudly than others. For example, the kiwi and strawberry might be more prominent than the green grapes or pear slices. With cheeses, the dominant flavor is greatly influenced by how the cheese was made. If the cheese was washed in beer as it aged, then the dominant flavor might be reminiscent of beer's ingredients (yeast, for example). If the cheese was made with milk that came from goats grazing on grass in lemon orchards, the dominant flavor may be lemony. In general, cheeses offer flavors of salt and milk, and often grass or hay as well.

Wines are trickier because they are incredibly complex beverages that may have a variety of flavors. For pairings, try to ascertain whether there is one that rises above the others. For example, Sauvignon Blanc often has a dominant flavor of citrus fruit, and South African Pinotages usually have a dominant flavor of cocoa. Because wine usually has acidity to it (which comes across as zippiness in white wine, for

Berries, apples, and spices represent some dominant flavors of wine.

example), the taste of sour can usually be found to some degree. If you're enjoying a dessert wine, white fruits may be readily detected.

Dominant Tastes: Does the food you're eating have a dominant taste? For example, oysters on the half shell are briny, making their dominant taste salty. Cotton candy's dominant taste is sweet. Lemon is sour, and so on. Remember the five basic tastes—sweet, salty, bitter, sour, and umami. When considering cheese, the tastes encountered most often are usually salty and umami. Cheese tends to be savory, although it's not crazy to come across a cheese on occasion that is a bit sweet.

Temperature: This is an easy one, right? Is the food you're eating hot or lukewarm? Cold? Cool? Notice the temperature because it plays an important part in the pairing. Think of ice cream, which is hopefully cold (otherwise, the "ice" part isn't really living up to its responsibilities). What would you drink with ice cream? Any beverage being consumed with ice cream would ideally be cold as well, such as a chilled dessert wine or even just a glass of ice water. Any room-temperature beverage will get lost in the pairing, not tasting like much at all. Hot beverages could be used as a contrasting temperature to the ice cream, such as in the classic Italian dessert *affogato*, which is a scoop of ice cream topped with a shot or two of hot espresso. The temperature of each is what really makes the combination interesting.

Foods often have dominant tastes and flavors.

The temperature of wine is important not only for the pairing, but for the enjoyment of the wine itself as well. White wine at room temperature isn't very appealing because tepid beverages aren't big on the refreshment factor, and refreshment is white wine's main appeal. Red wine that is too cold doesn't taste like anything, and red wine that is too warm can be overpowering and unpleasant. When thinking about the temperature of the wine for the pairing, think about what the wine is trying to accomplish. If you're enjoying a Camembert en croûte (wrapped in puff pastry and baked), do you want the wine to be a chilled, refreshing sip to counter the heat of the cheese? Or is the wine meant to be more of a companion to the cheese, in which case a glass of cool red wine may be just the thing.

Texture: The texture of food is often overlooked by people, except by those for whom texture is a big deal. I love texture. When I eat yogurt, I always mix in granola to give it crunch. When I eat pear slices, I usually add a bit of peanut butter or caramel for the rich, smooth texture. For other people, texture can be a less pleasant experience. Some people cannot eat mushrooms because of their texture, for example. When it comes to cheeses, there is a broad range of textures you may experience. Triple-crème cheeses are soft and spreadable. Manchegos are harder and drier. Gorgonzola naturale can be crumbled; mozzarella di bufala cannot.

Wine, while it has a texture as everything does, has a much smaller range of textures. It's a liquid, and so the main textural difference is viscosity—the thickness of the wine. Fortified wines are thicker and more syrupy than Chardonnay normally is. One exception to texture is astringency. As mentioned in chapter 1, astringency is a textural sensation that leaves your mouth dry and sandpapery after a sip. It is important to consider astringency because its characteristics are offset (quite nicely) by the presence of fat or salt in the food you're eating.

Foods have a broad range of textures.

Star anise, chili pepper, peppercorns, cinnamon, and nutmeg are some of the spice flavors you'll encounter.

Wine is also affected by spice. The more intense it is, the duller your sense of taste can become. You won't get much from your glass of mellow Pinot Noir after a bowl of five-alarm chili. A stronger, more assertive wine such as red Zinfandel from California or Priorat from Spain can stand up to the intensity of the food. Most wines aren't naturally spicy. There are drinks made with wine, however, that can be. German glühwein is red wine mulled with spices and served hot. It's delicious in the wintertime, and pairs well with a number of German soft cheeses, largely because of the spices in the wine.

Spice: As the foods of the world become easier to come by, we are exposed to a much greater variety of ingredients from heretofore exotic locales. Many of these newly experienced ingredients are spices and peppers from Africa and Asia, and they are turning up more and more in recipes and restaurant dishes. When considering your ingredients, take note of any spiciness. Chile peppers, peppercorns, even spices in quantity such as nutmeg, can have a huge impact on your sense of taste.

Cheeses are generally not spicy. On occasion, a cheesemaker may dabble in spice, but it is not common. Pecorino di Pienza al pepperoncino, for example, has dried chile peppers mixed in with the curds, and even our old pal Pepper Jack has a similar bite to it. Otherwise, spice is uncommon in cheese.

TANNINS, FAT, AND SALT

Tannins in red wine leave your mouth feeling dry and sandpapery after each sip. The more tannins, the stronger these impressions are. Those impressions play well with fat and salt. This is the idea behind "red wine with steak." Most cuts of red meat are marbled with fat to varying degrees (filet mignon has virtually none, whereas rib eyes are loaded with marbled fat). Additionally, steaks are usually prepared with salt and fat in the form of butter or oil. When these ingredients mix with tannins in your mouth, the sandpapery feeling turns to velvet and smoothness, a very pleasant effect.

PICKING A STRATEGY: TO CONTRAST OR COMPLEMENT?

One of the best ways to consider a pairing is to think about the foods and beverages as either contrasting or complementing each other. These two strategies for pairing provide a huge range of options with which to work. The first step is to recognize your own preferences.

If you think of all the foods you like or dislike, you can weave a thread through them and come up with common characteristics. It may sound odd, but it's true. It's important to become aware of your preferences and dislikes. In doing so, you'll make pairing decisions that better suit your palate. For example, I don't like truffles. Never have. They taste like greasy mushrooms to me, and any food containing more than a hint of truffle in it produces for me such an oppressive aroma that it's almost unbearable. Same with foie gras. The cloying and thick nature of this globally revered food is too much for me. I get no enjoyment from eating it, and so I generally don't. In my line of work, this is often considered sacrilege by my peers. To not like truffles and foie gras is to (obviously) not like fine foods at all, I'm told. Doesn't bother me in the least. When you find what works for you, stick to it. After all, you're the one eating it!

When it comes to food preferences, people tend to fall into one of two camps of ingredients. This isn't to suggest one can only be in a single camp—almost always people find appealing food characteristics in both categories. It's just that more often than not, there is a clear preference.

It's alright not to like some flavors, even truffles.

TRY IT!

A Pinch of Salt, a Sip of Wine. Here's a simple way to experience the magic that is tannins mixing with salt. All you need are a few sips of a medium-bodied or bold red wine and a pinch of table salt. In quick succession, take a sip of the red wine, taste the salt, and then take another sip of the wine. The first sip of wine coats your mouth with tannins and gives an initial impression. The salt interacts with the existing tannins and is sensed by your tongue, and the second sip of wine mixes it all together for a final impression. Depending on your sensitivity to salt, you probably noticed the wine seemed smoother and silkier, as if the "volume" of the tannins had been turned down!

Members of "Camp A" prefer flavors such as lemons, chili pepper, vinegar, white wine, and citrus fruit.

Members of "Camp B" prefer flavors such as chocolate, cinnamon, and red wine.

Camp A. People in this group prefer bright and lively flavors. They usually like fresh fruits, especially citrus. They may prefer mustard or vinegar on their fries instead of ketchup. Often, these folks like spicy foods, enjoying the peppery bang that jalapeños or crushed red pepper flakes add to foods. They tend to like white wines, and usually prefer their beverages cool or chilled instead of hot (for example, they would prefer an iced coffee to a hot one). In general, the people in this group like foods and drinks that are stimulating, peppy, and maybe even a bit sassy.

Camp B. The people in this camp prefer big, rich flavors and textures. For them, heaven is pasta in a thick ragù, with a goblet of red wine to sip on. Their fries get ketchup or even gravy. Dark chocolate is usually a favorite, as is a cup of hot, dark roast coffee. For them, red wine is the go-to choice, and the bolder the better. People in this category prefer foods and drinks that have weight and body, boldness and impact.

Even with these distinctions, it can be difficult figuring out where one's allegiances lie. To simplify, let's have a drink and sort it out.

Lemonade or Chocolate Milk?: Imagine you're thirsty. In front of you are two choices: a glass of sweet and tart lemonade, or a glass of rich chocolate milk (or regular milk, if chocolate isn't your thing). Forget the season and even the time of day. All things being equal, which glass are you reaching for? What if you did it a hundred times: how would the ratio play out? Think about it for a moment, because your answer reveals a lot about your preferences.

I reach for lemonade every single time. One hundred percent. Now, I do enjoy chocolate milk quite a bit, but there will never be a single time it beats out lemonade for me. Whether dead of winter or scorching heat of summer, the crack of dawn or the middle of the of night, it's lemonade! Clearly, I'm a member of Camp A. Knowing that, is it surprising that I love spicy foods? Or that I drink more white wine than red? Or that my single favorite flavor in the entire world is lime? It makes sense, right? Everything I just mentioned shares the same frisky and zippy characteristics.

My wife, Carmen, is somewhere around 80 percent chocolate milk. She very much aligns herself with Camp B. When she eats pasta, she

All the elements of macaroni and cheese complement each other in texture and flavor.

In a salad dressing, the viscous and rich olive oil contrasts with the acidic tang of the vinegar.

loves a full-bodied tomato sauce. Chocolate is a weakness for her. When she drinks coffee, anything less than the darkest roast mankind can offer is scoffed at. As for her preference in wines, let's just say if I could figure out a way to liquefy a chainsaw and put it in a glass, she'd gladly quaff it down.

It may seem silly thinking about your tastes in terms of milk and lemonade, but it suggests a pattern in your preferences. Once that pattern is recognized, better choices can be made for pairings that will make you happy. Knowing this will help you choose your pairing strategy.

Here's the secret: the more "lemonade" you are, the more you probably enjoy contrasting elements in your food pairings. The more "milk" you are, the more you like complementary elements. Complementary? Contrasting? What do I mean by that? Glad you asked.

The Odd Couple—Contrast versus Complementary: When you are considering what to make for dinner, or even what to order off a restaurant menu, you are subconsciously considering whether to eat complementary or contrasting

foods. The best example I can give of a complementary dish is macaroni and cheese. Everything about this classic comfort food is pushing in the same direction—the cooked pasta, the béchamel sauce, the melted cheese, and the toasted breadcrumbs. (Even the little bits of hot dog if you've had a bad day.) All of it is harmonious as you chew it. People find pleasure in food combinations that are similar in texture and weight. Complementary pairings create a unified impression when eaten. The ingredients in fettuccine Alfredo are all complementary. Fish and chips are complementary as well—the batter-fried fish and the oily fries are best friends because they share characteristics.

When too much macaroni and cheese has been eaten, it's salad time. Oil and vinegar dressing on the salad is a fantastic example of contrast. The coating, buttery notes of the olive oil are offset by the acidic tang of the vinegar. They balance each other out in a way that is pleasing to eat. There are many examples of contrasting elements in pairings. Sweet and sour is very popular, and found quite often in foods. Another trendy combination is salty and sweet—caramel with sea salt is a favorite. These pairings use contrast to excite the palate.

There are many ways to add a particular taste to a pairing. If you're looking for some more salty tastes, add capers or anchovies to the plate.

DECIDING WHAT TO USE

Once the main characteristics have been identified and the strategy selected, it's time to pick the ingredients to use. As with pairing in general, this may seem overwhelming because there are so many options!

If the pairing calls for something salty, for example, you could use capers packed in salt, or anchovies, or even just plain salt. There are many ways to add a salty taste to your combination. The trick is to select an ingredient that will enhance the pairing overall, not just blindly add the taste or flavor you're looking for.

Let's say you have a lovely wedge of French Brie. It's soft and creamy, with delicate flavors and a melt-on-your-tongue texture. Let's also say you want to enjoy this with a French Muscadet—a white wine from the Loire Valley that has bright citrus notes, but also a note of salinity from growing near the ocean. You want to find an ingredient that will bring them together in a delicious way. The cheese has a bit of salt, and the wine has a touch of citrus. Anchovy might be considered because it is salty and found in the sea, tying it to the wine a little, but fish and cheese is a tricky game, and often doesn't end well. Instead, maybe consider mincing up some preserved lemons (lemons soaked in brine for a month or so). Aging the lemons softens the rind and makes it edible, but keeps that bright, lemony flavor that is perfect for the wine. It also has a saltiness from soaking in the brine. That saltiness is found in the cheese and is reminiscent of the wine—a great common ingredient to bring them together. More specific pairing ideas are discussed in the following chapters.

PICKING THE STAR OF THE SHOW

One of the most common mistakes made in pairing is trying to have both the food and the wine be the "star" of the pairing. The logic goes something like, "If I'm serving a fancy wine, I should serve a fancy meal with it." In doing so, the guest eating and drinking is forced to consider two noteworthy items instead of focusing on one. Remember, there can be only one center of attention at a time. If you're serving a complex and sophisticated meal, keep the wines simple and let the food claim the spotlight. If the wine is a stunner, keep the accompanying foods simple and uncomplicated.

MOST IMPORTANTLY . . .

The single most important lesson I teach is so simple and obvious, it's almost ridiculous—eat and drink what makes you happy! No matter how outlandish the combination may seem, no matter how loudly the "experts" rail against your choices, if you like it, do it.

My father is the best example of this philosophy. My dad truly enjoys exactly one wine in this world—a $17 Merlot from California. Loves the stuff. It's made by a large producer that makes hundreds of thousands of cases each year. It's not a particularly fancy Merlot, but it's a reliably enjoyable bottle of wine. There are, however, two aspects to my dad's wine-drinking habits that are a little bit challenging for me to accept as a wine professional. He keeps the wine in the refrigerator all the time, and once a bottle is opened, it's the only bottle he'll drink until it's finished. When I bring my son Max over to his house to play with Papa this weekend, he'll offer me a glass of wine. With head hung low and a sigh (because I know what's coming), I'll accept. With a smile, he'll dash off to the kitchen and return with a juice glass filled with ice-cold Merlot that is somewhere around three months old. My dad doesn't drink a lot of wine.

As a wine nerd and dutiful son, I've tried for years to share some of the great Merlots of the world with him in the hopes of broadening his horizons. I would bring different bottles to holiday gatherings, his birthday parties, special occasions—anywhere an opportunity arose. My greatest attempt came on his sixty-fifth birthday. For his celebratory dinner, I brought a $400 bottle of Bordeaux. It was a top-notch bottle of Merlot. The wine showed delicate aromas of blackberries and flowers. The flavor was rich and layered, with a finish that lingered seemingly forever. It was, in a word, sublime. Proudly, I presented a glass to my dad (a proper vessel, not a juice glass), confident I had finally succeeded in my mission—to find another Merlot he would enjoy just as much as his old standby. He tasted it, and gave a single-word review: "Eh." Eh! He had just sipped one of the best Merlots on the planet, and it did not impress him one bit. He eschewed this magnificent Bordeaux for the wine he truly enjoyed. I was so proud of him. He gets it, even if by accident. His enjoyment of wine isn't driven by cost, or by what someone else tells him is a great wine. He likes what he likes, and he unapologetically drinks that. Bravo, Dad!

A FINAL THOUGHT

Palates are like snowflakes—each one is unique. Your tongue grew up differently than mine did. It experienced different things and developed different preferences. When trying these wines, cheeses, and combinations, remember that your own palate has its own likes and dislikes. What sings for one palate is painfully out of tune for another. The secret isn't to learn to like what I like. It's to discover your preferences, and love the heck out of them! In wine and cheese pairing, one flavor definitely doesn't fit all, and that is a glorious thing.

This chapter touched on basic pairing concepts. As I mentioned earlier, once these are internalized they can be applied to almost everything you eat and drink, and your dinner parties will never be the same. But we're here to talk wine and cheese in particular. The next chapters focus more closely on wine types and what to eat with them. Let's get pairing.

(3)

SPARKLING WINES

Ahhh, the joys of a glass of bubbly. Who doesn't like the festive sight of tiny bubbles cascading upward in a fluted glass? Or the way these wines tickle the nose and stimulate the palate? Everyone loves a glass of sparkling wine. The very sound of a cork popping, the sight of the distinctively thick glass bottle with the foil-wrapped neck, means a celebration is near. Believe it or not, that association with celebrations is partially the problem. We're so busy toasting occasions with these magnificent wines that we miss what makes them truly special—their amazing ability to pair seamlessly with foods. And cheese. Especially cheese!

When was the last time you had a glass of sparkling wine? Any sparkling wine, whether it was Cava or Prosecco or even a singularly regal Champagne? Was it in celebration of some event or occasion? Probably, and you're not alone. The world over serves these wines above all others when something celebratory happens, and it's not surprising. The sound of the cork, the action of the bubbles, the refreshment of every sip seems to say "party!"

When it comes to sparkling wines, most people have it all wrong. Although these wines are the best around at adding a little something special to a celebration, they are often overlooked for the amazing food-friendly partners they are. Those same festive bubbles that make people giggle are the same bubbles that brilliantly serve as palate cleansers for a wide array of foods. From the richest cream reduction to the sharpest cocktail sauce, sparkling wines can raise the pairing game to the next level.

As rewarding as sparkling wines can be when well paired with foods, they can be a bit maddening to select. What is the difference between Cava and Prosecco? Are all sparklers Champagne? Where do the bubbles come from? With which cheeses are they best served? Excellent questions! On to the basics of bubblies.

THE BASICS OF SPARKLING WINES

Sparkling wine is an interesting animal, one that begins life the same as any other wine. Crushed grapes yield juice filled with sugars that are converted into alcohol. Unlike other wines, however, sparklers enjoy a bit more pampering. After all, the bubbles don't make themselves. Or do they?

WHAT MAKES THEM SPARKLE: A TALE OF TWO TECHNIQUES

Fundamentally, sparkling wine is still wine (noncarbonated) that has been infused with carbon dioxide. This carbonation creates bubbles. The origins of sparkling wine are buried in legend. Effervescence was recorded in ancient Greek and Roman writings, but any kind of understanding where the bubbles came from didn't arise until the mid-seventeenth century, when a British scientist named Christopher Merret presented research making the connection between the presence of sugar in a wine and resulting bubbles. This new ability to intentionally carbonate a wine created a whole new style of wines for people to enjoy!

There are two main ways to create bubbles in wine, the traditional method (also called the Champagne method, or *méthode Champenoise*) and the Charmat method. Both methods start with the same fermentation of grape juice— using yeasts to turn natural sugar into alcohol. The traditional method adds a second, much smaller fermentation in the bottle (called the secondary fermentation), and the bubbles are captured instead of being allowed to escape. The Charmat method also involves a second fermentation, but it occurs under pressure in large steel tanks, and then the wine is bottled. This way is a little more cost-effective for the winemaker, and is not subjected to the rigorous laws the traditional method must abide by. Part of the winemaker's job is to determine how much sugar is to be used, and of that sugar, how much will be converted into alcohol. Any sugar *not* fermented into alcohol stays in the wine and makes it sweeter.

DOM PÉRIGNON— FACT OR FICTION?

Mention sparkling wine, and inevitably the name Dom Pérignon is invoked. Many people incorrectly attribute the creation of sparkling wine to him, chalking it up to the vagaries of legend. There was indeed a monk named Dom Pérignon who lived in Champagne, France, in the seventeenth century. At the time, Champagne was making still wines (noncarbonated wines) that were mostly red. He was tasked by his superiors to figure out a way to prevent bubbles from forming in the bottles in the Abbey of Hautvillers' wine cellar because trapped carbonation made the bottles unstable, and they would often explode. Dom Pérignon actually spent most of his life trying to eliminate bubbles! The contributions from his research largely shaped the future of sparkling wine production.

SPARKLING SWEETNESS

Most sparkling wine labels have an adjective identifying how sweet the wine inside is (or isn't). For many people, this description may be a little confusing. Is extra-dry sweeter than brut? Which is the sweetest? The driest? It can be more than a little confusing. There are five basic levels of sweetness in sparkling wines.

Brut Nature: This is the driest wine made, meaning it has the least sugar left in it. All the sugar has been consumed during fermentation, and so none is left in the wine.

Extra-brut: These sparkling wines are at their best with foods that are rich and have some fattiness to them. There aren't too many extra-brut wines on the market. They are around, but nowhere as popular as brut or extra-dry wines.

Brut: This is the most popular and common style of sparkling wine. The winemaker stopped fermentation just before all the sugar was consumed, and so a little remains in the wine, making it taste just the tiniest bit sweet. Of all the sparkling wines, Champagne is the one most often categorized as brut.

Extra-dry: From the name you might think this style of sparkler would be, well, extra dry. In fact, it is slightly sweeter than brut because the winemaker stopped fermentation even a little bit earlier than in brut, leaving a bit more sugar in the wine. If you sipped a brut wine next to an extra-dry wine, you would immediately sense the difference. Spanish Cava and Italian Prosecco are most often made this way.

Demi-sec: The sweetest of the styles, demi-sec has enough sugar left in the wine to make it noticeably sweet. These sparkling wines are usually enjoyed with dessert because they have the weight and sweetness to pair well with desserts.

The sweetness level of a sparkling wine is important because it helps determine what kind of food it is best paired with. The sweeter the wine, the heavier or sweeter the accompanying food can be as a complement. The drier the wine, the more contrast it will provide against rich and creamy cheeses it encounters. Sweetness is one of several factors to consider when pairing.

PAIRING WITH CHEESE

The whole point of a sparkler is to enjoy a wine that is effervescent, lively, and full of fun. These wines also have fruity, bready characteristics that make them great choices for a variety of foods. When it comes to cheese, there are a couple of general guidelines to consider. As with any of these pairing ideas, ultimately do what makes you happy!

CONSIDER THE DRYNESS OF THE WINE

The drier the style of wine, the more contrast it will provide to cheeses that have softer, creamier interiors, especially double- and triple-crème cheeses. The more sugar left in the wine, the more complementary it will seem when encountering cheeses with softer and richer interiors. To complement a dry sparkler, pair it with a cheese that has less fat in it. A fresh goat cheese, for example, would be *très* complementary to the sharp and angular flavor of the wine.

CONSIDER THE BUBBLES

Higher-grade sparkling wines typically have smaller bubbles that last longer than their lower-grade counterparts. These bubbles play an important part in your enjoyment of the wine because smaller bubbles feel creamier and smoother on your tongue. Think of the difference between any sparkling wine and taking a sip of carbonated soda. The wine has much more elegance to the fizz than the cola, right? It's all about tiny bubbles.

BETTER BUBBLES

The better the sparkling wine, the better the bubbles. Higher-quality sparkling winemakers spend more time and care to create a better-made wine, and small bubbles (collectively called the *mousse*) are a sign of that effort. A bottle of well-made Champagne, for example, can produce up to 250 *million* bubbles! Better wines will also produce bubbles for a longer time. Cheaper carbonation methods (like soda pop) produce larger bubbles, which dissipate much more quickly.

These considerations are helpful once you've determined the kind of sparkling wine to be enjoyed. Now let's look at some specific sparkling wines and the cheeses that create really delicious pairings.

CAVA

Once called "Spanish Champagne" because it is made the same way as the famous French bubbly, this refreshing and food-friendly sipper is an important part of Spanish (especially Catalan) traditions and culture, almost always being served at celebrations and parties since it's mid-nineteenth-century creation. Cava can range from dry to sweet, with most being sold today in the dry style.

THE WINE

Cava is made from several different grape varieties, but is typically made from Xarel-lo, Macabeo, and Parellada. Even though it is made using the same process as its more famous French counterpart, Cava is quite different to drink. Unlike the sharp, angular qualities of Champagne, Cava is more easygoing and approachable, with aromas of apples, flowers, nuts, and sometimes an herbal hint. The wine is light and zesty, with flavors that can be a little lemony with pears and melons, and sometimes a touch bitter like green almonds as it finishes.

THE CHEESE THAT LOVES IT

Cava's bright and zesty flavors and sharp bubbles make it a perfect partner for cheeses with a higher fat content and fuller flavor. Try a young Arzúa-Ulloa (cow milk, Spain). The soft, pliable interior and grassy notes are perfect for the wine's freshness. Firmer cheeses with fruity characteristics also pair nicely because the wine's creamy texture and light fruitiness elevate the cheese's nutty, fruity flavors. Try Gruyère Alpage (cow milk, Switzerland), especially with some dried apricots to really make the fruit connection sing.

MATCH MADE IN HEAVEN

Leonora (goat milk, Spain) with fresh pear slices. This striking cheese has tart flavors mixed with a lovely earthiness that brings out the zestiness of the wine. The fresh fruit adds a mild flavor that bridges the wine and cheese deliciously, and the pear's soft acidity keeps the pairing refreshing.

FACT

More than 95 percent of Spain's Cava production comes from Catalunya (Catalonia in English). Although bars and restaurants all over Barcelona serve a wide variety of producers, there are two main competitors in the market for your sipping attention: Freixenet and Codorníu.

CHAMPAGNE

The standard by which all other sparkling wines are compared, Champagne is the worldwide winner for popularity, to the point where most sparkling wines are simply called Champagne. Made from three grape varietals, this regal sparkling wine can be made in styles ranging from bone-dry (brut nature) to sweet (doux), with most producers opting for the drier versions.

THE WINE

Champagne can only be made from three grapes— Chardonnay, Pinot Noir, and Pinot Meunier. Each grape adds a different characteristic to the blend—Chardonnay adds delicacy and freshness, Pinot Noir brings complexity and body, and Pinot Meunier adds fruitiness and floral aromas. Some producers choose to make their wine with only one grape. All-Chardonnay Champagnes are called Blanc de Blancs ("white of whites"), and all-Pinot-Noir wines are called Blanc de Noirs ("white of blacks," referring to white wine made from the dark Pinot Noir grape). Frequently, the wine you're enjoying is a blend of all three grapes. Champagnes are elegant and sophisticated, with aromas of brioche, white flowers, peaches, and toasted nuts. Flavors can vary greatly, but typically include green apple, freshly baked bread, almonds, marzipan, and often faint dark berries. Champagne is a fantastically complex wine, and is best paired with mild cheeses that don't challenge the wine.

THE CHEESE THAT LOVES IT

Mild cheeses are best for pairing with this wine. The texture is less important, although it's undeniably more fun to eat creamy and soft cheeses and then take a sip of wine, letting the bubbles clear away the cheese. Try the soft and sweetly melting Coulommiers (cow milk, France). This French Brie has a somewhat salty interior with a pleasing yet slight funkiness to the flavor that emphasizes the wine's bready qualities. For a more complex flavor, try the truffle-studded Sottocenere al Tartufo (cow milk, Italy). The rich, earthy tones of the truffles and the softness of the cheese bring out the texture of the wine.

MATCH MADE IN HEAVEN

Langres (cow milk, France) and a dry Champagne. This cheese is named for the village in Champagne from which it originated. A small cylinder, Langres is firm and supple, almost melting in your mouth. Aromas and flavors of fresh cream and mushrooms are common, making this cheese a great companion to the wine. In fact, this cheese has a slight indentation on the top (called a *fontaine*), which is meant to be filled with Champagne! The wine coats the cheese with each bite, making this an elegant way to enjoy both.

CRÉMANT

Sparkling wines made outside the French region of Champagne are not allowed to use the famous name. Even though they may be made the same way, tradition prevents them from benefiting from Champagne's recognition. Made elsewhere in France, these intriguing wines tend to be softer and creamier than Champagne. Approachable and thoroughly enjoyable, Crémants are a great alternative to their high-priced northern counterparts.

THE WINE

Imagine a Champagne with softer bubbles and less attitude. Every bit as enjoyable, Crémants are youthful and energetic. The Blanc de Blanc Crémants have aromas of citrus and minerals, mixed with flavors of fruits like apple and apricot. Blanc de Noirs Crémants have more power and structure, with aromas and flavors of blackberry and raspberries and the occasional hint of nutmeg. These wines love cheeses that are rich and creamy.

THE CHEESE THAT LOVES IT

Cheeses that have a soft texture and complex flavors work well with the wine's youthful energy. Try a Chaource (cow milk, France). The double-crème interior is moist and cakey with hints of mushroom. For a more savory combination, try the aged Comté Fort Saint-Antoine (cow milk, France). A French Gruyère aged for ten to fourteen months, this cheese is dense and solid, with a beautiful fruitiness that blends with the wine's character really well.

MATCH MADE IN HEAVEN

Délice de Bourgogne and fresh blackberries. This triple-crème cheese is unbelievably creamy, almost spreadable. The flavor is milky and slightly salty. This cheese is all about the hedonistic pleasure of eating it. The wine's refreshing bubbles cleanse the palate each time and add a freshness to the pairing. The blackberries' dark fruity tone marries the cheese and wine fantastically, especially when chilled.

FACT

Crémant, which means "creamy," is often used in naming French sparkling wines not made in Champagne (which get to use the famous name). It was the name originally used because the wines generally had lower amounts of carbon dioxide in them, giving them a creamy mouthfeel.

LAMBRUSCO

With a name translating as "wild grape" in its native northern Italian tongue, Lambrusco might be expected to be a powerhouse reeking of earth and leaves. Nothing could be further from reality. Lambrusco is a collective name representing up to sixty different varieties of grapes, and every single one of them wants to party.

THE WINE

This wine's bright ruby red color and intense aromas of red berries entice you to take a sip. Virtually always made as a sparkling wine (which only adds to the refreshment and fun quotient of this wine), Lambrusco is made in varying levels of sweetness, ranging from secco (dry) to dolce (sweet). The bubbles are not as sharp and aggressive as those of sparkling wines made in the style of Champagne. A different fermentation and carbonation technique is employed, which results in softer, gentler bubbles the Italians refer to as *frizzante* ("frizzy").

THE CHEESE THAT LOVES IT

This wine screams for rich, opulent cheeses with a high fat content. The softer and richer, the better. Try Gratte-Paille (cow milk, France) or Robiola Tre Latti (cow, sheep, and goat milk, Italy) and let the frizz gently refresh your palate after every bite.

MATCH MADE IN HEAVEN

For quite possibly the greatest brunch combination in the known world, serve well-chilled Lambrusco with whipped ricotta mixed with berries and a light drizzle of acacia honey. The light, refreshing milkiness of the cheese and the viscosity of the honey are the perfect dance partners for the zippy acidity of the wine and the berries.

FACT

Throughout the 1970s and 1980s, Lambrusco was the top-selling imported wine in the United States. In the Emilia-Romagna department of Italy, there are five regions allowed to use the Lambrusco designation in their name. The largest is Lambrusco Reggiano, which is also the region most responsible for exporting this delicious wine to the United States.

MOSCATO

A member of the yellow-skinned Muscat family, the Moscato Giallo grape is often turned into a lightly carbonated wine that is a little sweet, a little fruity, and a whole lot of fun. Lower alcohol levels and a sunshiny disposition make Moscato a fantastic choice for brunch, sipping at parties, and pairing with light foods.

THE WINE

The grape usually used for this wine, Moscato Giallo, is hardly grown outside of northeastern Italy. As with all wines made from members of the Muscat family, Moscato shows a fresh, grapey aroma and flavor. When made well, Moscato will also have notes of baked apples, orange peel, and citrus in general. The carbonation is milder than that of many sparkling wines, and is called *frizzante* ("frizzy") by Italians. The bubbles are a little larger and softer, resulting in a wine that is easier to sip straight up during cocktail hour.

THE CHEESE THAT LOVES IT

Because the wine has such a fresh personality, it's best to keep the cheeses simple and easy—too much aging or character will overpower the fun-loving wine. Try Fontal Nazionale (cow milk, Italy). This mild and semisoft cheese is milky and creamy, with just a touch of salt. Both fresh and aged goat cheeses also work well because their mild flavors accent the wine's freshness. For fresh cheeses, try the intriguing Tronchetto Caprino al Miele (goat milk, Italy). Brushed with honey as it ages, it develops just the right amount of complexity for the wine to complement. For aged goat milk cheeses, a favorite is Pantaleo (goat milk, Italy). The aging mellows out the sharp edges of the cheese's flavor, but it keeps the slight lemony note that makes it a winner with Moscato.

MATCH MADE IN HEAVEN

Fresh burrata and chilled grapes. If you're not familiar with it, burrata ("buttery" in Italian) is a "purse" of fresh mozzarella with a filling. Originally, it was butter, cream, and sugar. Modern versions usually use fresh cheese curds or pureed figs. The light and creamy notes of the cheese pair perfectly with the wine's fresh grape flavors. What better way to bring them out even more than with fresh, chilled grapes? This combination is fun and playful.

FACT

Meaning "musky" in Italian, this aromatic grape has been around a long time. The name first appears in Piedmontese documents dating back to the thirteenth century, and is known as one of the oldest grapes grown in that area.

PROSECCO

Made from the highly productive Glera grape, Prosecco is fast becoming the worldwide favorite when sparkling wine is called for. Often called "sparkling joy," this northern Italian wine is game for almost any party. Flavorful, lower in alcohol, and unpretentious, Prosecco is a great choice for pairing with a wide array of cheeses. Or foods. Or by itself!

THE WINE

Prosecco styles range from dry to sweet, with many being made more toward the dry end of the scale. It is crisp and refreshing, with a clean and focused zippiness, and aromas of Meyer lemons and apples are common, as are grapefruit and pears. Prosecco has a milder and more approachable flavor and texture than the more austere Champagne. Softer bubbles and sweeter flavors heighten its drinkability. Sometimes these wines can have a slight bitterness to them, which only increases their compatibility with cheeses.

THE CHEESE THAT LOVES IT

Prosecco can work with both soft and creamy cheeses, and aged and salty ones as well. The softer cheeses work great because the sharp bubbles cleanse the palate, setting it up for another bite. Try the sinfully creamy Pavé d'Affinois (cow milk, France), a small, brownie-sized cheese that is gooey in the middle with just the right amount of salt. Aged cheese works well because the more intense flavors and saltiness counter the wine's softer notes. Try a piece of classic Parmigiano-Reggiano. Fresh goat cheeses make for a delicious Sunday morning snack with some grilled bread. Try fresh chèvre from your local supermarket. The simple, tangy notes of the cheese bring out the energy of the wine and keep it light.

MATCH MADE IN HEAVEN

Reblo Cremosa with grilled peaches. This square cheese is lightly washed as it ages, giving it an orange rind and a soft, unctuous interior that is mild and creamy. Grilling slices of fruit causes the sugars to burn just a little, making those beautiful char lines. The peaches have a similar weight as the cheese, making it a pleasure to chew. The wine's racy acidity keeps it from getting too heavy.

FACT

Prosecco is often enjoyed as an affordable alternative to Champagne. Unlike its French counterpart, however, Prosecco does not ferment or age in the bottle (it is fermented under pressure in tanks and then bottled). Because of this, most Proseccos are best enjoyed young, ideally within three years of the vintage.

SEKT

Made in the same way as Prosecco, this German sparkling wine doesn't get the attention it deserves, largely because of so many bad past examples. Fortunately, better versions of Sekt are becoming easier to find and enjoy.

THE WINE

Made from a variety of grapes including Riesling, Pinot Blanc, Pinot Gris, and Pinot Noir, Sekt juice is often brought in to Germany from France, Italy, and Spain, although better producers are now exclusively using German grapes. Delicately effervescent, Sekt is sweet and has aromas of apples, pears, and white flowers, and sometimes hints of wood. The flavors are full of white grapefruit, tart apple, and usually peaches.

THE CHEESE THAT LOVES IT

Sekt's sweet and bright profile makes it a great choice for cheeses that have a soft interior and mild notes. Try Jasper Hill's Moses Sleeper (cow milk, United States). This Brie-style cheese has a gooey, milky interior with gentle aromas of mushroom, toasted nuts, and sometimes cream. The flavor can range from grassy and lactic when young to more savory notes of cauliflower as it ages. For a fun, salty-sweet contrasting pairing, try a goat milk feta cheese. Sharper than sheep milk versions, goat milk feta has a simple flavor and aroma that centers on salinity from the brine the cheese is made and stored in. The simple and clean flavors will work nicely with the wine's sweetness.

MATCH MADE IN HEAVEN

Anton's Liebe Rot with wildflower honey. This washed-rind cheese is made from organic cream and has a mildly aromatic rind. The interior has flavors of hazelnuts and mushroom, with a lingering finish that sweetens at the end. The honey adds a delicate, floral note to the aroma, bringing out the floral notes of the wine. The honey's sweetness bridges the cheese and wine, making for a full-bodied combination that isn't too heavy. Delicious.

FACT

There is evidence of German sparkling wine production going back as far as 1826, when a former worker from Veuve Clicquot began making wines, calling them "Mousseux," "Sect," or "Champagner." This practice continued until the Treaty of Versailles in 1919, which expressly forbade Germany from using these names. From then on, the generic term "sekt" was used, a term coined in Berlin.

(4)

WHITE WINES

It is amazing how often people default to red wine for their cheese pairings. What about white wine? It is true that white wines tend to be simpler than red wines, usually being served chilled or at least cool. It's also true they generally don't have the same aging potential of red wines. But they do have a secret weapon—they are often more nuanced and approachable than red wines, and pair every bit as well with foods. On the whole, they may not have the same horsepower as red wines, but that is completely, totally okay.

White wine tastes best when it is chilled, not cold. A common mistake is to drink white wine right out of the fridge, as most refrigerated beverages are (an "ice cold" soda or beer is around 35°F [1.7°C]). The colder the beverage is, the "tighter" the flavors are, and the more difficult it is to sense and enjoy them. If you're pouring a crisp white wine, aim for 40° to 50°F (4.4° to 10°C). Full-bodied white wines like oaked Chardonnay benefit from a higher temperature, ideally between 50° and 60°F (10° and 15.6°C).

THE BASICS OF WHITE WINE

White wines begin, as all wines do, as grape juice. They are fermented the same way as red wine, but unlike red wines, the skins are not used once the grapes are pressed for their juice. The "red" in red grapes comes from a pigment in the skin of the grape. (So, all grapes yield the same color juice.) The difference is juice for red wines is fermented with the red skins soaking in the liquid. Heat from fermentation causes the pigment to bleed out and stain the wine red. White wine has no such concern. Once the juice is extracted, the skins are removed from the process (okay, a few makers still add them for flavor complexity and whatever, but I'm keeping it simple here). Fermentation takes place, and then it is aged.

If the wine is oaked, that aging happens in oak barrels, where the wood fibers add character and a second fermentation may take place to turn tangy, green-apple malic acid into milky, smooth lactic acid. (Cleverly, this is called "malolactic fermentation.") Unoaked wines go right to the filtering and final bottling stages.

The process is actually rather straightforward. With each step, however, come myriad decisions the winemaker must make that will steer the developing wine one way or another, ultimately coming to the wine's final expression. Once the wine's personality is revealed, the fun of pairing foods to that wine can begin.

PAIRING WITH CHEESE

Pairing white wine with cheese is all about identifying the wine's characteristics, and deciding which are most important to you. Characteristics like acidity, dominant flavor, and body are important. Is the wine bright and crisp, like a New Zealand Sauvignon Blanc might be? Does it have rich vanilla aromas that are found in many California Chardonnays? Does it have fuller body and a touch of sweetness like some German Rieslings?

Once you pick out these personality traits in the wine, the next decision is whether to complement these characteristics or to contrast them. Bright, tangy goat cheeses will be perfectly complemented by an Italian Orvieto, but would be contrasted by the fantastically oily texture of a French Semillon from Bordeaux, especially one that is demi-sec (semisweet). Medium-bodied cheeses like Camembert play nicely with wines that have a little more body to them, especially with those that have oaking. French Chardonnay would work wonders here.

Soft cheeses like bright acidity found in wines such as Grüner Veltliner or Sauvignon Blanc. Heavy cheeses like oak and body—Chardonnay, anyone? Stinky, washed-rind cheeses love wines with a little residual sugar, like that found in Gewürztraminer. Blue cheeses need viscosity and floral notes, like those found in French Vouvray or Sauternes. These general guidelines can help in a pinch, but let's take a look at some specific pairings.

ALBARIÑO

This green-skinned grape is also known in northern Portugal as Alvarinho. In Spain, this aromatic grape constitutes more than 90 percent of the vines planted in the Rias Baixas wine region, and is one of the top go-to white wines for people looking for refreshing simplicity.

THE WINE

Bright and lively, Albariño wines often have aromas that are floral and quite fruity, with notes of orange peel, bergamot, and grapefruit and hints of linden flower and lemongrass. Flavors of acacia honey, peaches, citrus fruits, and honeysuckle work perfectly with the fresh acidity for a well-balanced wine that is refreshing and food-friendly. Versions from Portugal's Vinho Verde region are often lightly carbonated and sold as Alvarinho. These are meant to be enjoyed when young, and as often as possible!

THE CHEESE THAT LOVES IT

Albariño is happiest with younger goat and sheep milk cheeses. For goat milk cheeses, try Ibores (goat milk, Spain). With its pimentón and olive oil–rubbed rind, Ibores features peppery and warm milk flavors that awaken the acidity in the wine and allow the fruity aromas to shine. Another excellent goat milk pairing is Leonora (goat milk, Spain). The cheese's simple interior and developed rind match the wine's aromatic body, creating a delightful combination. For a fuller-bodied pairing, try Three Corner Field Farm's fresh sheep-milk Shushan Snow (New York). The cheese's soft and creamy interior has just the right amount of tang for the wine. Avoid blue cheeses with this wine.

MATCH MADE IN HEAVEN

Albariño with Garrotxa St. Gil (goat milk, Spain) and bergamot preserves. The cheese has some aging to give it a mellow flavor and chewy texture—just the right conditions for the wine's rich fruit notes to blossom. The acidity in the wine combines with the citrus flavors of the preserves to contrast the weight of the cheese while keeping the whole experience light and refreshing. This is a great combination for a lazy Sunday brunch in the sun.

ASSYRTIKO

Greece's most iconic grape is gaining popularity outside the Mediterranean, and will continue to do so. This versatile and intense wine comes in a variety of styles ranging from fresh and minerally to the deeply nutty and rich tones of the dessert wine Vin Santo.

THE WINE

When made into a young, dry wine, aromas of apple and citrus blossom appear, and have a great minerality to them, along with just a tinge of sea air. These wines are perfect for the cuisine of the islands, and are valued for their ability to keep their acidity, even in the extreme heat. For this wine, acidity equals refreshment during the hot, humid summer days.

THE CHEESE THAT LOVES IT

Cheeses with creamy, soft textures work well because they are contrasted by the wine's zippy acidity. Try Nettle Meadow's Kunik Button, a creamy blend of goat and cow milks. The cheese is buttery and a touch sour on the finish with hints of salt. For a firmer cheese, try pairing Assyrtiko with Sicilian ricotta salata, a simple and basic sheep milk cheese with a slightly chewy texture (that still crumbles well) and a salty finish.

MATCH MADE IN HEAVEN

Of course, feta! Sheep milk feta will give a richer, fuller texture to the cheese, and the salinity of the feta makes the Assyrtiko sing. Mix the cheese with grilled shrimp, kalamata olives, really fresh oregano, and roasted tomatoes. Add a bottle (or two) of chilled wine, and bask in the sun! A superb summer combination.

FACT

Although cheese production in Greece is evidenced as far back as the eighth century BCE, *fetta* cheese as we know it isn't documented until the late fifteenth century, when an Italian visitor noted sheep and goat milk cheeses made into slices and stored in brine. The Greek name "feta" comes from the Italian word *fetta*, meaning "slice," a term first introduced into the Greek language in the seventeenth century. Before then, Greeks called this wonderful cheese *prósphatos*, meaning "fresh."

CHARDONNAY

One of the most popular wines in the world, Chardonnay grapes are planted virtually everywhere wine is made. Born in Burgundy, France, this somewhat neutral-flavored grape can be turned into wines of unmatched splendor and elegance, or reduced to cheap wine barely worth the bottle it's sold in.

THE WINE

More than almost any other grape, Chardonnay has characteristics that are largely influenced by the terroir in which it is grown and the technique of the vintner. Unoaked Chardonnays, best represented by northern Burgundy's village of Chablis and many new-world Chardonnays, show aromas and flavors that are sharper and edgier. These wines usually display notes of citrus, especially lemon and lime, and may have a chalky aroma as well. At times, they can smell like wet rocks and on occasion are reminiscent of Sauvignon Blanc, especially when the Chardonnay has a strong aroma and flavor of green apple.

THE CHEESE THAT LOVES IT

Unoaked Chardonnay is quite flexible with cheeses. If you prefer to complement the minerally and citrusy flavors of the wine, a fresh goat cheese is perfect. Try the classic Valençay Frais (goat milk, France). This truncated pyramid was a favorite of Napoleon, and when you taste the chalky, tangy cheese with the wine, it will be one of yours as well! The ash rind on the cheese ever so slightly emphasizes the chalky characteristic of the wine. For a contrast pairing, enjoy this crisp, zippy style of Chardonnay with the simple and unctuous Pavé d'Affinois (cow milk, France), a double-crème cheese that oozes flavors of cream and a touch of saltiness. This combination is a textural treat.

MATCH MADE IN HEAVEN

Blue Ledge Farm's Lake's Edge (goat milk, United States) with a drizzle of orange blossom honey. This cheese's gorgeous interior is cakey and rich, with a striking line of ash running through the center, and has a clean, lemony flavor. The citrus honey adds a lovely aroma to the combination, and the body of the honey contrasts the zip of the wine. Another brunch winner!

CHENIN BLANC

Born in Anjou, a village in France's Loire Valley, Chenin Blanc is still best known as a Loire wine, although South Africa now makes outstanding Chenin Blancs as well under the varietal name Steen.

THE WINE

A vastly important grape to the Loire wine industry because of its flexibility and quality, Chenin Blanc is used in sparkling wines (especially the delicious Crémant de Loire), and is the grape for the glorious wines from Vouvray and Saumur, where they range from bone-dry to richly sweet. Dry Chenin Blancs have aromas of green apple, white flowers, and honey, and can be quite aromatic. The flavors are similar, with a rich body and a roundness to the wines that make them amazing food wines.

THE CHEESE THAT LOVES IT

Goat cheeses are an easy choice. Try the amazing Tronchetto Caprino al Miele (goat milk, Italy). This stout cheese is brushed with honey for the short time it ages, giving the cheese an amazingly complex aroma and flavor that is part goat milk, part honey. For a more opulent combination, pair dry Chenin Blanc with a cheese that has more milk fat in it to really make the fullness punch out. Try Brillat-Savarin (cow milk, France), a triple-crème cheese that is lusciously rich and creamy. This combination is all about the pleasing texture of the pairing.

MATCH MADE IN HEAVEN

Selles sur Cher (goat milk, France) with lemon preserves and a dry Chenin Blanc, ideally from Vouvray. This combination is almost too perfect—the cheese comes from the same neighborhood as the wine. They grew up together and work together perfectly. The bright, lemony notes of the cheese seamlessly meld with the honeyed notes of the dry Chenin Blanc. The lemon preserves add another layer of citrus tang, but also sneakily add body to the pairing because of the sugars. This is one of my favorite combinations!

FACT

Wine expert Jancis Robinson noted Chenin Blanc may be the world's most versatile grape. It can be made sweet or dry, sparkling or still, meant to consume young or suitable for aging. She suggests it may be France's answer to Riesling.

GEWÜRZTRAMINER

One of the most aromatically recognizable wines in the world, this "spicy Traminer," as the name translates, is often mistaken for Riesling, as both are full-bodied and highly aromatic, as well as loved and disdained by many. Gewürztraminer is at home in Alsace, France, although New Zealand, the Pacific Northwest of the United States, and northern Italy make great bottles as well.

THE WINE

Gewürztraminer is unique in the wine world. A relatively low-acid wine (especially when tasted alongside a well-made German Riesling), it features the aromas of lychee, petrol, and rose petals, a unique profile indeed! The wine's flavor profile is no less interesting. Common flavors include peach, mango, apricot, and often a slight spicy note of ginger. These wines are full and textural, and the low acid can make them seem a little syrupy. That characteristic makes it a winner with soft, full-bodied cheeses that have lots of character themselves.

THE CHEESE THAT LOVES IT

This wine wants to be paired with cheeses that have intensity of flavor and aroma. Yes, that means the stinky ones! Washed-rind cheeses are fantastic partners for this equally aromatic wine. Try Hooligan (cow milk, United States) or Ardrahan (cow milk, Ireland), and see how well the wine tames the flavors of these aggressive cheeses. If you just can't bear the thought of a stinker, try a flavorful, aged cheese, such as a reserve Parmigiano-Reggiano.

MATCH MADE IN HEAVEN

Muenster, Muenster, Muenster! Especially Muenster from Alsace, France. The cheese's rich, buttery interior plays well with the wine's body, and the assertively aromatic washed rind is matched in strength and intensity by Gewürztraminer's huge aromas. While not a subtle combination in any way, for those who like their music loud, this is fun.

GRÜNER VELTLINER

An offspring of the Traminer grape, Grüner Veltliner is Austria's signature white wine. Growing in popularity, "Grü-Ve" is popping up on restaurant wine lists and in wine shops more and more often, and with good reason. This crisp, spicy wine is winning people over one glass at a time.

THE WINE

There are two basic styles made. The first is light-bodied, with bright and tangy acidity and a clear preference for citrus aromas and flavors. The second style is more concentrated and complex, with spicier aromas of black pepper and deeper fruit tones. These wines are surprisingly suitable for aging a few years.

THE CHEESE THAT LOVES IT

Younger Grüner Veltliners are best with bright, simple cheeses that mirror the wine's flavors. Try a young Sainte-Maure Belgique (goat milk, Belgium), whose slight milky sourness on the finish complements the wine nicely. For a more complex wine, try a young sheep milk cheese like Saveur du Maquis (sheep milk, Corsica). The herb-crusted rind adds a delightfully herbaceous complexity that matches the wine's deeper notes. Both styles of Grüner Veltliner are contrasted nicely by richer, creamier cheeses like Brie (cow milk, France), or Robiola due Latte (cow and sheep milk, Italy).

MATCH MADE IN HEAVEN

La Tur (cow, sheep, and goat milk, Italy) with lime marmalade. The cheese is all about the rich texture and slightly sour finish. The interior is firm, but the cheese has a certain airiness to the texture that is delicate and almost sweet. Marmalades utilize citrus rinds to achieve that bitterness that accompanies the sweetness, and lime is the perfect flavor to bring out the same notes in the wine. The marmalade's bitterness emphasizes the wine's minerality rather nicely!

FACT

Although there is evidence Grüner Veltliner has been around since Roman antiquity, the name was not first documented until 1855. Before then, it was known as Weißgipfler. Ampelographic research suggests Grüner Veltliner may be related to Pinot Noir as either a grandchild or half-sibling.

MUSCAT

Thought to have originated in the Middle East, the Muscat grape family is one of the oldest in the world with over two hundred members, and is thought to get its name from the musky aroma similar to that of the male deer musk used in fifth-century southern Asia to make perfumes. Muscat thrives in hot climates and favors the Mediterranean locales of Italy, France, and Spain.

THE WINE

Most easily recognizable as Italian Moscato d'Asti, Muscat Blanc is enjoyed particularly because of the wine's bright, grapey flavor (making it a popular snacking grape as well). This also causes the wine to come in a variety of styles ranging from sparkling to dry to sweet. The Muscat grape often has aromas of citrus fruits, white flowers, and just a little spice. The flavor is mostly that of fresh grape juice, with a touch of fresh melon. Muscats are not suited for aging. They want to be consumed as young as possible!

THE CHEESE THAT LOVES IT

The simple grape flavors and bright fruitiness of the wine lends itself to a variety of pairing options. To keep it simple and light, pair it with fresh ricotta (cow milk, locally made) and some chilled green grapes. For a more interesting pairing, serve this well chilled with a mild blue cheese such as Fourme d'Ambert (cow milk, France). The bright grape flavor works well with the saltiness of the cheese. Creamy blue cheeses also work well because the wine's acidity cuts through the additional body of the cheese. Try Gorgonzola dolce (cow milk, Italy).

MATCH MADE IN HEAVEN

Bayrischer Blauschimmelkäse (cow milk, Germany) with apricots in syrup. This über-mild blue cheese is rich and creamy, with buttery flavors and an almost melt-in-your-mouth texture. The wine's fresh fruit notes match the cheese's mildness well. Apricots in simple syrup add a bright, fruity note that wakes the wine up even more, and adds to the full mouthfeel of the cheese and wine.

PINOT GRIGIO

One of the most popular wines in the United States, Pinot Grigio is the Italian designation for Pinot Gris, the same grape grown in France. The difference? Pinot Grigio wines are typically light and crisp, while the French-named counterpart is usually heavier and more complex. Fortunately, many more interesting versions are available beyond those served with fried onions and sour cream dip in shopping-mall chain restaurants!

THE WINE

Pinot Grigio is the pinnacle of refreshment. The clean and simple aromas and flavors make this wine a favorite for serving as an aperitif. Aromas of white flowers, citrus (especially lemon), and green apples abound, with sharp flavors of lemon and apple and a quick, easy finish. Pinot Grigio is a very easygoing wine to sip.

THE CHEESE THAT LOVES IT

Because the wine is so simple and refreshing, keep the cheese pairings equally as basic. To complement the bright citrus notes, a fresh goat cheese is superb. Try Cornilly (goat milk, France) or Vermont Creamery's Coupole (goat milk, United States). For a contrasting pairing, try Brebirousse d'Argental (sheep milk, France), an unctuous and gooey cheese with lovely notes of cream and salt.

MATCH MADE IN HEAVEN

The freshest ricotta you can find (cow milk, locally made) mixed with dried apricots and a dash or two of freshly ground black pepper. The simplicity of the cheese is a kindred spirit with the wine's refreshing quality. The contrast of sweet, dried apricots with the bite of the black pepper adds depth to the pairing, but keeps the overall impression light and not too serious. For a fantastic dinner pairing, mix this combination in with freshly cooked linguine and just a touch of the pasta water to turn the cheese into a simple sauce. This combination is a staple on my summer dinner table. Amazing.

RIESLING

Considered by some to be the greatest white wine in the world, Riesling is misunderstood by many as only a thick, viscous dessert wine. Not true! Although Riesling is made in a rich, honeyed style, the majority of Rieslings are dry and complex, making for some of the best food-pairing wines in the world. Because it is not grown in France, Italy, or Spain, Riesling has to work harder to gain the trust of wine lovers. Those who do, however, are richly rewarded!

THE WINE

At its finest in Germany, this light-skinned and highly aromatic grape yields juice that is loaded with sugars. When fermented, these sugars transform Riesling into a wine with magnificent aromas ranging from peaches and apples to spices, pineapples, and tropical fruits. The lush and opulent flavors of white fruits, honey, orange, mango, and sometimes white pepper are intoxicating. Because the wine has a greater amount of fermented sugars, the feel of Riesling in the mouth is different—fuller, rounder, more viscous—but not necessarily sweeter! Rieslings are made with varying degrees of sweetness—ask your favorite wine nerd for a little help navigating. Riesling is spectacular with spicy foods because the weight and richness of the wine calms the heat of the spices. Try a glass the next time you add wasabi to your sushi.

THE CHEESE THAT LOVES IT

Pair with cheeses that have body and weight. Try Morbier (cow milk, France), the classic washed-rind cheese with a soft and flavorful interior with a layer of ash. Washed-rind cheeses are right at home with Riesling's huge mouthfeel and bright acidity. If you like 'em stinky, try an authentic Limburger (cow milk, Germany) with pickles and raw (yes, raw) onion slices. For those who are a little less adventurous, pair a dry Riesling with the mild and delicious von Trapp Oma (cow milk, United States). While still a washed-rind cheese, Oma has a much milder aroma and sweeter flavor. Medium-bodied cheeses like Gruyère, Cheddar, and Tomme de Savoie (cow milk, France) also work well.

MATCH MADE IN HEAVEN

Winnimere (cow milk, United States) with toasted hazelnuts, a spot of light honey, and a dry Riesling. The combination of toasted nuttiness, sweet honey, and orange peel from the wine are amazing with the rich, lactic aromas and creamy mouthfeel of the cheese. This combination is big and satisfying, and can be served as a dessert on its own.

SAUVIGNON BLANC

Once thought of as a simple wine, this expressive and fun grape is finally getting the appreciation and admiration it deserves. Born in Bordeaux, France (and a parent to Cabernet Sauvignon), Sauvignon Blanc now has a second distinctive style from decades of cultivation half a world away from France, in New Zealand, where it makes amazingly zesty and aromatic wines.

THE WINE

Old-world French Sauvignon Blanc can be serious and austere, with aromas and flavors of mineral, lime peel, flint, and sometimes underripe fruits and asparagus. New-world "savvy," as it's sometimes called, takes itself far less seriously. Sunny aromas and flavors of grass, citrus, gooseberries, and pink grapefruit keep the mood light and playful. Both versions have racy acidity, making Sauvignon Blanc a great complementary choice for cheeses that are light and simple, and a great contrast to cheeses that are rich and creamy.

THE CHEESE THAT LOVES IT

Ash-rinded goat milk cheeses have just a touch of chalkiness to them that is perfect for old-world Sauvignon Blancs (especially from the Loire village of Sancerre). Try Sainte-Maure de Touraine (goat milk, France), a classic Loire Valley cheese made in the shape of a log, with tangy, lactic notes and a pleasing sourness to the finish. Sauvignon Blanc also pairs well with fuller-bodied cheeses that are mild in flavor. Try Brebis Abbaye de Belloc (sheep milk, France). The fuller body and sweet milky flavors of the cheese pair well with the lighter notes of the wine.

MATCH MADE IN HEAVEN

For some textural fun, pair the wine with a triple-crème cheese such as Gratte Paille (cow milk, France) and some dried guava. The cheese has a lick-your-plate level of salty, creamy flavor, and the guava adds a tangy fruit note. Sauvignon Blanc's bright, zesty acidity cuts right through the richness, resetting your palate for the next bite. And the next. And the next!

TORRONTÉS

One of Argentina's most important grapes, Torrontés is virtually synonymous with Argentinian white wine. With large berries and thick skins, this grape prefers vineyards at high altitudes, where arid, hot days give way to chilling nights, bringing out the best in this aromatic beauty.

THE WINE

Highly aromatic and big on refreshment, Torrontés wines can range from light and fresh to complex and heady. Oak is hardly ever used, preserving the wine's acidity and crispness. The aroma can be quite complex, with notes of peach, fresh herbs, and flowers. The flavors can include citrus fruits (especially oranges), peaches, and sometimes a slight spiciness. Torrontés is big enough to handle cheeses with a little bit more weight and flavor to them, yet is zingy enough to pair nicely with fresh goat and sheep cheeses.

THE CHEESE THAT LOVES IT

Simple cheeses such as *mozzarella di bufala* (buffalo milk, Italy) keep the pairing deliciously light and refreshing, with a clean finish. For a more complex experience that is still easy to appreciate, try Serra da Estrela (sheep milk, Portugal). This cheese approaches Brie in texture, but with buttery, grassy flavors and a washed-rind complexity that won't overpower the wine. Hard cheeses can work too, as long as they have a bright flavor to them. Try Pantaleo (goat milk, Italy), a cheese with flavors that are slightly herbal with just a hint of pepper.

MATCH MADE IN HEAVEN

Monte Enebro (goat milk, Spain) with a daub of rosemary honey. The cheese has an ash rind and a smooth, white interior. The flavor is slightly tart and has a mild saltiness and gentle earthy notes. The rosemary honey brings sweetness and body, but subtly emphasizes the herbal qualities of the cheese and wine.

FACT

In Argentina, the name "Torrontés" is used for three different grape varieties. Torrontés Mendocino (which has the smallest, tightest grape clusters of the three), Torrontés Sanjuanino (a more loosely-clustered grape vine with stronger, more aromatic qualities), and the most popular, Torrontés Riojano.

TXAKOLINA

This Spanish Basque wine is just now catching on in the States. Also known as Txakoli or Chacolí, Txakolina (pronounced sha-KO-leena) is young and fun, and with its refreshing bubbles, it is far easier to drink than pronounce.

THE WINE

With a bright, lively character and a short life span in bottle (around a year), Txakolina is low on alcohol and big on refreshment. Most are white, although red and rosé wines are made in smaller quantities. With a slightly green tint in the glass, Txakolina is fresh and lightly fizzy, making it a great wine with cheeses. Bright acidity keeps it sharp, and aromas of lemon, lime peel, and minerals keep it simple. Txakolina has flavors that are citrusy and tangy, especially lime.

THE CHEESE THAT LOVES IT

The crisp, bracing acidity of the wine makes it the perfect wine to contrast double- and triple-crème cheeses, by cutting through the thick mouthfeel of the cheese to reset the palate for the next bite and sip. Try Robiola Tre Latti (cow, sheep, and goat milk, Italy). The cheese's full body and simple, clean milk flavors are contrasted beautifully by the wine's zip. Goat milk cheeses do well also. Try the aged Garrotxa St. Gil (goat milk, Spain), from the Catalan region of Spain. The semi-firm interior is delicate and milky, with a hint of nuttiness. Fresh cheeses like ricotta and sheep-milk feta cheese are also great ideas here.

MATCH MADE IN HEAVEN

Leonora (goat milk, Spain) with lime marmalade and white Txakolina. This whole combination is tangy and fruity. The wine and marmalade bring lime notes to the pairing, which works well with the cheese's slightly sour finish. The richness and sweetness of the marmalade pairs nicely with the cakey Leonora, and both are contrasted by the wine's crispness and bubbles. A fantastic combination!

TREBBIANO

Doing business as Ugni Blanc in France, this little-recognized grape is the most widely used white wine grape in Italy as the only grape allowed to be used for balsamic vinegar, and also France, where it is the main grape for making Cognac and Armagnac.

THE WINE

Wines made from the grapes of the Trebbiano family are usually fairly simple and straightforward, making them easy to enjoy. Aromas of citrus and flower blossoms are common, with some more complex wines adding tropical fruits to the profile. Trebbiano has flavors of lemon and lime, and a pleasantly mild nuttiness in some versions. These simple characteristics make this wine a great choice for cheeses that are as laid-back as the wine.

THE CHEESE THAT LOVES IT

Cheeses with mild flavor are best, as strongly flavored cheeses will overpower the wine. Try Monte Veronese Latte Intero (cow milk, Italy). The cheese's semisoft interior is milky and a touch sweet with a slight bite as it finishes. Fresh cheeses like mozzarella and queso fresco would also work well, especially with a spoonful of lemon preserves. Harder cheeses pair well as long as they aren't too strongly flavored. Try Pecorino di Pienza Morchiato (sheep milk, Italy), a firm pecorino with a rind that is rubbed in olive pomace as it ages. The slightly nuttier flavor is a flavorful complement to the wine.

MATCH MADE IN HEAVEN

Fresh chèvre with a little grated lemon peel and some Ligurian olives. The simple, creamy brightness of the cheese is contrasted by the mild saltiness and buttery oil of the olives. The wine keeps the brightness of the goat cheese while standing up to the salinity of the olives.

VERDICCHIO

*Best known as the white table wine from Italy's central Marche region,
Verdicchio has been around since the fourteenth century, although some evidence
suggests even a hundred years before that. It is also found in northern Italy,
and often mistaken for the similarly mild Italian wine Trebbiano.*

THE WINE

A slight yellow-green in color, Verdicchio is mildly aromatic with notes of lemon peel and nuts. This wine is uncomplicated and fresh, with bright acidity and lovely flavors of lemons with a bitter almond finish. It's this bitterness that makes it a fantastic cheese wine when paired with mild and creamy cheeses or cheeses with a nutty flavor. Well-made Verdicchio wines may also have hints of apricots, anise, and even a touch of smokiness.

THE CHEESE THAT LOVES IT

Cheeses with a semi-firm texture and nutty flavors work well. Try Fontina Val d'Aosta (cow milk, Italy), with its soft and mild interior. The Brie-like Mount Alice (cow milk, United States) from von Trapp in Vermont gives the cheese a pliable texture and simple, milky flavor to play with. Fresh goat cheeses pair deliciously as well, making a refreshing and vibrant combination. Try the beautiful, leaf-wrapped Castagnino (goat milk, Italy).

MATCH MADE IN HEAVEN

Cornilly (goat milk, France) with lemon marmalade. This goat cheese is simple, tangy, and delicious. The texture is cakey, with lots of moisture that makes it almost smearable. The notes of lemon bring out the same flavors in the wine and marmalade. The bitterness of the marmalade ties in with the slightly bitter finish of the Verdicchio, and the marmalade's sweetness brings it all together.

FACT

The name Verdicchio is thought to have derived from the Italian word verde, meaning "green," referring to the grape's greenish-yellow hue on the vine. So often is it confused with the similar looking grape Trebbiano. Though there is some evidence Verdicchio may be related to Trebbiano, they are certainly not the same wine.

VIOGNIER

Made from the eponymous grape, Viognier has a reputation for being a bit difficult to grow and make wine from. Its thick skin means the grape needs lots of sunshine to develop properly, and naturally has low acidity. Despite these challenges, this aromatic and full-bodied white wine from France is now made all over the world, and is even considered a specialty of Virginia!

THE WINE

Viognier is known for being particularly aromatic, with aromas of lavender, ginger, and white stone fruits. Low acidity gives the wine an impression of fullness and richness on the tongue. Flavors of apricots, honey, and sometimes dried herbs pair with a typically "steely" finish.

THE CHEESE THAT LOVES IT

Try the opulent Brillat-Savarin (cow milk, France), a triple-crème cheese from northern France. The simple, creamy interior provides the perfect complement to the wine's body and mellow acidity. Because of the wine's strength, a rich washed-rind cheese also pairs well. Try Livarot (cow milk, France). This cheese is washed in light brine as it ages, giving it a bit more horsepower in aroma and flavor. The cheese's nuttiness and soft texture work well with the Viognier.

MATCH MADE IN HEAVEN

Port Salut (cow milk, France) and acacia honey. This popular cheese is so soft and yielding that it often sticks to the knife when cutting it. Wrapped in cloth as it is aging, the cheese sometimes retains the cloth pattern on the rind. Like the Viognier wine, Port Salut has low acidity, matching the body of the wine nicely. Acacia honey complements the full-bodied character of the cheese and the wine.

FACT

The exact origins of the Viognier grape are not entirely known. Current research suggests it originated in Dalmatia (current day Croatia) somewhere around the first century. Even the name's origin is shrouded in mystery. One theory suggests the name comes from the pronunciation of "via Gehennae," Italian for "road of the valley of hell."

White wine is most enjoyable when chilled, not cold.

OAKED WINES

When vintners make wine, a world of possibilities opens to them. Each decision they make throughout the entire process, from the grapes they plant right down to the type of cork they choose to seal their bottles, plays a part in the outcome of the wine. The French call this collective influence terroir, and it is a significant part of what makes wine such an amazing beverage. Two different producers can use the same grapes and make two hugely different wines. One important decision is whether to oak the wine or not. Oaking adds a distinctive characteristic to wine, and may be employed by a vintner to achieve a certain result.

For people starting to learn about wine, the subject of oak can be confusing. Is oak a good thing or a bad thing? Is it necessary? What exactly does it do? How does it work? To add to the confusion, many wine professionals and enthusiasts have very strong opinions on the topic that may conflict with other experts' opinions. Trying to make sense of it all can seem a bit overwhelming. To oak or not to oak? That is a really good question!

WHAT IS OAKING?

"Oaking" is the process by which wines are fermented and aged in barrels made of oak specially prepared for that purpose. It is an important, and often overlooked, part of winemaking. Why does oaking matter? In many cases, oak simply makes the wine taste better. The added flavors and textures oak provides can make the difference between a simple, uninteresting wine and one with layers of nuance and complexity. When vintners decide to use oak, they are usually making that choice because they want their wine to benefit from the additional flavors and aromas aging wine in oak brings.

WHAT DOES OAK DO FOR THE WINE?

Oak adds flavors and complexity to a developing wine, as well as naturally filtering it. Exposure to oak releases certain compounds into the wine, enhancing the aroma and flavor. These compounds add tones of vanilla, caramel, spice, and sometimes smoky or charred notes. The intensity of the effect depends on what kind of oak barrel is used, how new or used the barrel is, and how "toasted" the barrel was when it was made. (The barrel interiors are exposed to open flame to char the surface, then cleaned off. That charring is what opens the fibers of the wood to allow wine to seep in and absorb the compounds.)

The wood for wine barrels comes mainly from three sources—France, the United States, and Eastern Europe. Each has a unique set of characteristics and will treat the wine a little differently. French oak tends to be subtler than American oak. Eastern European oak is usually somewhere in the middle. Whichever oak is selected, the winemaker uses that barrel to enhance the wine.

HOW TO PAIR CHEESE WITH OAKED WINES

When considering a cheese to go with that oaked wine, focus on how much body the wine has and what the primary flavors are. Often, oaking imparts aromas and flavors of vanilla, spices, toffee, and sometimes a smoky quality. Usually, oaked wines have also undergone malolactic fermentation, which turns the wine's sharp, green-apple malic acid into soft and milky lactic acid, giving the wine a fuller body that seems almost creamy. This additional fermentation is what gives oaked Chardonnays their opulent texture and slightly sweet aromas.

The more oaking and malolactic fermentation that has occurred, the more intense those aromas and flavors will be, and the cheese will need to be able to keep up. Where a young, ash-rinded goat cheese would be delightful with a crisp, unoaked Chardonnay, it wouldn't be able to hold up when paired with a fully oaked version. In that case, a fuller-bodied double-crème cheese like Brie would be a much stronger pairing. Or, a cheese with more aging that still has fruity flavors could be enjoyed. Swiss Chällerhocker, with its heavy weight and amazingly complex flavors of toasted nuts and hay, would be fantastic with the oaked wine's creamier texture.

In general, the bigger the oaking, the bigger, fuller, or richer the cheese may need to be. In the end, though, pairing cheese and wine is an inexact science, if a science at all. Every person is different and perceives combinations in his or her own unique way. As a pro, I find it maddening to hear pairing advice that involves words like "always" or "never." When it comes to this stuff, never say never.

THERE ARE NO ABSOLUTES!

As you consider these pairing suggestions, keep in mind some of these wines come both oaked and unoaked. Oaking is often at the discretion of the winemaker unless otherwise called for or prohibited by the local wine laws. Pinot Grigio from northern Italy can be found oaked, an unusual find to be sure. Unoaked Chardonnay is nearly as prevalent and popular as the classic oaked expressions found in France and California. Gewürztraminer is usually made in an unoaked style, but not always. There are exceptions to wine rules everywhere. In the world of wine, the only absolute is there are no absolutes!

(5)

RED WINES

Red wine's heft often pairs well with the aromas and flavors in many cheeses. But what about milder, fruitier red wines? Do they provide the same broad appeal as their more burly counterparts? How about softer, creamier cheeses? Can red wines still make for a delicious duo, or will they overpower the cheese? With more red wine choices becoming available in shops and on restaurant lists, it's time to look at pairing red wine and cheese a little bit differently.

For many people, red wine is the go-to choice for pairing with pretty much any cheese. It's almost automatic, and it's understandable why. Red wine usually has a fuller body and makes a bigger impression when you drink it than white wine does. These characteristics typically play well with a wide range of cheeses, especially those as full and intense as the wine being sipped. What is often overlooked and left unconsidered, however, is the huge variety of styles in which red wine can be made. Rioja, Beaujolais, Chianti, and myriad others have their own voice and personality. There are so many wonderfully expressive wines that come from red grapes, and it's impossible to cram all their different characteristics together into a single descriptor as woefully blunt as simply "red wine." Unfortunately, people tend to group them all together without much consideration, and that can make for a lesser pairing that leaves the taster disappointed. A red Bordeaux may be bold and intense—the perfect partner for a slice of equally robust blue cheese like Roquefort, but not so much when paired with an opulently rich double-crème cheese that melts in your mouth. The softer texture and milder flavors would go much better with a gentle, fruity Pinot Noir, perhaps from Burgundy.

Pairing cheese with red wine can be quite rewarding. Once you select the cheese to enjoy, picking a red wine is a matter of considering the characteristics of the cheese you've selected, and what wine (or wines) will bring out the flavor and texture combinations you'll enjoy the most.

THE BASICS OF RED WINE

Red wines are some of the most complex beverages we consume. There are hundreds, if not thousands, of compounds comprising the aromas and flavors in a glass of red wine. Although most people don't think even for a second about 2-methoxy-3-isobutylpyrazine and a human's sensitivity to this compound (to the tune of ten to twenty parts per *trillion*), they certainly enjoy the fresh bell pepper aroma it lends to their glass of well-crafted Cabernet Sauvignon. And that's not a bad thing. Wine is best contemplated and mused, not overthought and dissected. The nerdy details of the chemistry involved may or may not interest you, but don't let them stand in the way of what is most important—when you take a sip of your wine, you smile and want to do it again.

Pairing red wine with food has come a long, long way as well. The archaic days of "red wine with red meat" and "white wine always with fish or chicken" are all but gone. As the body of food and wine pairing knowledge grows, and the culinary world becomes more accessible to everyone, the old pairing logic becomes less and less relevant. Food and wine lovers are experimenting with bolder ingredients and combinations, and loving them. So, too, is the art of wine and cheese pairing evolving. It was not all that long ago that Chianti was the only wine one would consider drinking with a chunk of Parmigiano-Reggiano, or a sip of port with the British blue cheese Stilton. These combinations are classic and stand the test of time, but they are just no longer the *only* way to go.

Parmigiano-Reggiano with Chianti is still a classic, but more options are now available than ever before.

Not only are people more willing to try new flavors, but the range of options is constantly increasing as well. There are now more red wine choices to consider than ever before. Twenty years ago, the choice was relatively simple—bold or mellow? Italian or French? Cheap or expensive? The lines are more blurred now. Outstanding values from South America can be found, where a little bit of money can buy a lot of wine. Delicious red wines can come from Turkey and Croatia, unheard of a decade ago. Even within single grape varietals, global variations in style and expression are more pronounced—Cabernet Sauvignon from Bordeaux is worlds apart from the Cabernet Sauvignon enjoyed in Chile. Same grape, different personalities.

Although it may seem a bit daunting to navigate such a vast sea of options, the benefits of such variety available to the everyday wine lover are wonderful. And, with a little bit of attention paid to what you like in a red wine, choosing the perfect wine for your needs becomes that much easier.

THINK DIFFERENTLY ABOUT RED WINE

Randomly ask wine drinkers what their favorite red wine is. Chances are, they'll answer with something like Cabernet Sauvignon, Pinot Noir, or Malbec. I ask this question of everyone who takes my classes, and I'm fascinated at the predictability of the answers. Merlot. Zinfandel. Syrah. The same responses over and over. What do all of these answers have in common? They are all names of grapes. Although this may not seem odd at first, identifying your favorite wines by grape varietal can prevent you from trying new and equally exciting wines because it keeps you relegated to the grapes you mention by name. People go in to their favorite wine shop hoping to try out something new, and instead find themselves sitting in their car minutes later with a bottle of the same old stuff, thinking *what happened?*

Instead of thinking of red wine in terms of the grape from which it was made, think of red wine in terms of the characteristics you experience when drinking it. Figure out what you like about the wine, and you can seek out alternatives that share those characteristics. Fruit, intensity, and flavor profile are all important. For red wine, there are two core characteristics to consider, old-world style versus new-world style, and how tannic the wine is.

OLD-WORLD STYLE
VERSUS NEW-WORLD STYLE

In the world of fine foods and wines, the descriptors "old world" and "new world" are bandied about a lot. They are trendy terms, and many people don't realize everything they may represent. Primarily, they refer to the geographic region from which a wine or cheese comes. "Old world" means pretty much what the name implies—old Europe, mainly France, Italy, Spain, Portugal, and Germany. "New world" in this context represents everyone newer to the wine and cheese party (relatively speaking)—the United States, South Africa, New Zealand, Australia, and others.

These descriptions also speak to the winemaking philosophies and viticultural practices each style employs. To many old-world cultures, wine is a food in itself, and it is at its very best when consumed with a meal. The thought of a glass of wine "just because" seems rather foreign; by all means have a drink before dinner, but make it a gin and tonic or vodka martini, perhaps. To the new-world mind-set, wine is a drink to be enjoyed whenever and wherever you please. Have a glass at brunch! Have a glass with friends at a bar! Have a glass on the ride to work! (Kidding. Don't do that.) The spirit of new-world wines is much more about the indulgence of the moment. These differences really can come through in the wines.

Old-world wines heavily focus on the tradition and terroir of the wine, and how prominently it comes through in the glass. Old-world wines consider the "whereness" of the wine as the driving factor, and that notion is subtly reinforced in the labeling of their wine bottles. Where many new-world bottles display the grape varietal, emphasizing the grape's characteristics, the majority of old-world bottles are labeled with the vineyard or region from which the wine came. This practice underscores the old-world philosophy that where the wine came from is more of a determining quality factor than what the wine was made from.

New-world vintners emphasize science and the role of the winemaker. They focus on how a wine was made, and the competency of who made it. The style of new-world wines tends to be higher in alcohol and may be fuller-bodied. Bottle labeling is more informative to the casual wine drinker, as it often tells the reader which varietal is in the bottle, saving the effort of having to research a place of origin to learn more about the wine. Terroir is a factor in new-world wines, but less of a priority than technique and winemaker experience may be.

TERROIR?

Terroir is a French word that means, roughly, "sense of place." It represents all the unique characteristics and variables affecting wine during every phase of its life from vine to bottle. Soil, climate, harvesting time, and winemaking methods are some of the factors "terroir" represents. Fundamentally, terroir assumes every variable in a grape's journey from vine to wine poured into a glass plays an important part in how the wine turns out.

IT'S ALL ABOUT THE TANNINS

What are tannins? The nerdy answer is tannins are phenolic compound molecules. Along with anthocyanins (another phenolic compound), they create the taste, color, and mouthfeel of red wine, and give red wine its healthful properties. The shorter, easier answer is tannins are compounds found in red wine largely responsible for that drying sensation you feel after taking a sip.

Tannins play an important role in the making and aging of red wines. They give the wine structure and body, and give wine the longevity it needs to age successfully. And they are often the main characteristic people notice in the red wine they're enjoying. Even if they can't put their finger on what a "tannin" exactly is, they know it when they taste it!

Tannins are found in plants, wood, seeds, leaves, and fruit skins. They exist in the skins of wine grapes, especially red-skinned grapes (white grapes do have tannins in their skins, but in extremely small quantities that aren't noticeable). They are perceived as a textural element—felt more than tasted. The more tannins present in the wine, the more bitter or astringent the wine may seem. The less tannic the wine, the softer and fruitier it usually seems.

When thinking about red wines, most people focus on the grape they're drinking, rather than the characteristics of the wine they are enjoying (or not). When it comes to pairing red wine with cheese, flavor is of course important. Equally important is how the tannins will blend with the cheese. Try thinking about the wine a little bit differently. Instead of focusing on the flavor, identify how strong the wine's tannins are. Looking at wine in this light will go a long way toward making a rock-solid pairing.

Tannins are found in the skins of red grapes and walnuts.

TRY IT!

Tannins can be a bit of a confusing concept. Fortunately, it's easy to experience tannins in a clear and simple way. Brew a cup of hot tea, and leave the tea bag in for fifteen minutes or so. Then take a sip. Notice that drying, puckering sensation in your mouth? Maybe it feels a little "sandpapery"? Those are tannins making that happen. Tannins are also found in the skins of walnuts.

PAIRING LIGHT- TO MEDIUM-TANNIN RED WINES WITH CHEESE

Red wines with light to medium tannins are everyone's pal because they are usually very easy to get along with and eager to please. Typically fruit driven, these wines can be lively and engaging. They can be chilled a bit to heighten refreshment, and generally play well with uncomplicated foods. If you're at a picnic and there's a pitcher or two of red wine on the table for people to sip on, it probably belongs on this team!

For red wines that are playful and easygoing, pair them with cheeses that are simpler in texture and flavor. Although these wines can be matched with bigger, bolder cheeses, they lose a little bit of their personality in the combination because they are the lesser element. The stronger cheese commands more attention, and the wine takes a back seat. Cheeses with softer textures and milder flavors are best suited for these wines.

RED WINE'S BEST PALS: FAT AND SALT

Red wine with steak, right? Ever wonder why that is? Sure, the darker tones of the wine match the rich beef flavors. But an even deeper magic is at work, and that is the reaction created when tannins are mixed with fat and salt. The animal fat and salt soften tannins considerably, making them seem smooth and velvety. It's a pleasant sensation, and at the core of that pairing logic. Just make sure the tannins in the wine are matched by the amount of fat in the meat. Filet mignon, while scrumptious, has little to no fat and therefore can't stand up to wines with big tannins, such as Cabernet Sauvignon. Rather, consider a wine with softer tannins such as Pinot Noir or Barbera. For cuts of steak like rib eyes that have lots of fat marbled in, pick a much more tannic wine such as Malbec, and it will pair well.

Steak and red wine are a classic combination (and with good reason).

BARBERA

Grown mostly in northern Italy, Barbera can also be found in the Americas and even as far away as Australia. This dark-skinned grape has ancient roots, and is thought to have originated in Piedmont around the thirteenth century.

THE WINE

Barbera's high levels of acidity are complementary to its bright cherry flavors. As the wine ages, the flavor turns to a bit more sour cherry, but remains lively. These dry wines are often tangy and zippy, making them very sippable.

THE CHEESE THAT LOVES IT

Cheeses that play nicely with the wine's fresh red fruit flavors are the best choices. Look for cheeses that have a touch of nuttiness to them, such as Piave Vecchio (cow milk, Italy). Barbera's high acidity also works well with softer cheeses that are simpler in flavor—the tang of the wine cuts through the richness of the cheese. Try the classic washed-rind Italian cheese Taleggio D.O.P. (cow milk, Italy).

MATCH MADE IN HEAVEN

A ripe and unctuous Robiola due Latte (cow and sheep milk, Italy) with a spot of sour cherry confettura. The cheese combines cow and sheep milks, making it mild and creamy. The sour cherry notes of the confettura contrast the rich texture of the cheese and highlight the cherry notes in the wine.

FACT

Barbera is known in Northern Italy by more than twenty different synonyms. Locals may refer to it as Barbera Mercantile, Barberone, Gaietto, Lombardesco, Pignatello, or Ughetta.

CABERNET FRANC

Born in the Loire Valley in France, this parent of the more popular Cabernet Sauvignon is fragrant, silky, and medium-bodied. This underappreciated wine is an excellent alternative to heavier red wines.

THE WINE

The classic French expression of Cabernet Franc is fragrant, with notes of black currant, violets, and sometimes graphite (think of pencil shavings). Old-world styles also show a hint of green bell pepper, while new-world versions tend to minimize this characteristic while emphasizing the fruity notes of the wine.

THE CHEESE THAT LOVES IT

Cabernet Franc benefits from cheeses that work with the gentler tannins than are found in its progeny, Cabernet Sauvignon. Cheeses that have body, but are not aggressive, will pair nicely. Try Montgomery's Clothbound Cheddar (cow milk, England) or a mild Crosta di Pane (cow milk, Italy) to provide the body the wine needs without over-powering the flavors of the wine. Goat cheeses, especially from the Loire Valley, emphasize the wine's fresh fruit characteristic and benefit from chilling the wine just a bit. Semisoft cheeses such as Port Salut (cow milk, France) contrast the wine's tannins nicely as well.

MATCH MADE IN HEAVEN

An old-world Cabernet Franc, particularly from the village of Chinon in the Loire Valley, with a slightly aged Chabichou du Poitou (goat milk, France) and fresh berries (especially black currants). The fresh fruit notes of the wine and berries are complementary to the acidity in the cheese. The wine's youthful tannins contrast the cakey texture of the Chabichou.

FACT

Because Cabernet Franc ripens earlier than its offspring, Cabernet Sauvignon, Bordeaux winemakers often plant Cabernet Franc as an insurance policy to protect themselves in case inclement weather damages their Cabernet Sauvignon crops near harvest time.

FRAPPATO

A light-bodied red wine from the southeastern corner of Sicily, Frappato is often blended with the island's heavier red grape, Nero d'Avola. Gaining popularity in America, it is becoming easier to find, and with good reason!

THE WINE

Reeking of raspberries and dried strawberries, Frappato is a bright, garnet-colored glass of fun and simplicity. Not meant for aging, this wine loves good food and company, and a lot of it.

THE CHEESE THAT LOVES IT

The simple and happy nature of this wine calls for a similar dance partner. Goat milk cheeses work well because their lively acidity isn't lost in the wine—rather, they work together to create a peppy combination. Try Humboldt Fog (goat milk, United States). Cheeses that are mild, soft, and pliable also pair well because their simple and pleasing texture serve as a foil for the bright fruit notes in the wine. Try Fresa (cow milk, Sardinia). With a soft texture and mildly tangy flavor, this is one of Sardinia's very few soft cheeses, and it can be eaten fresh or even quickly fried.

MATCH MADE IN HEAVEN

This pairing takes a bit of preparation, but it is so worth it. Slice fresh strawberries, put them in a bowl, and sprinkle a little sugar over them. Mix in a few splashes of Frappato, cover the bowl, and let it sit in the fridge overnight. Then, pour them over the simple and salty Ricotta Salata (sheep milk, Sicily). The sweet berries now have a touch of boozy deliciousness to them, and it works magic with the salt in the cheese.

FACT

This Sicilian grape has a genetic makeup strongly similar to the Calabrian grape Gaglioppo. Although it was first thought to have come from Greece, modern DNA profiling has determined it is indeed of Italian origin.

GAMAY

Formally known as Gamay Noir, this grape is most commonly found in French Beaujolais. A prolific grape that calls Burgundy home, Gamay yields wines that range from cheap date to thoughtful conversationalist.

THE WINE

The simplest of the wines, Beaujolais Nouveau ("new Beaujolais"), can be a bit thin and "bubble gummy" if not made well; otherwise, it is bright and refreshing, with dominant red fruit flavors. Better-crafted examples (Beaujolais-Villages and especially Cru Beaujolais) are more balanced and complex, although they are not capable of extensive aging and development quite like Pinot Noir and Cabernet Sauvignon are. Satisfying flavors of dark cherry and often hints of black pepper make this light-bodied wine a perfect choice for casual consumption and celebrations alike.

THE CHEESE THAT LOVES IT

Soft and mild cheeses pair well with Beaujolais's easygoing nature. Brie (cow milk, France) will lend flavors of milk and grass to the wine's bright fruit. For a bit more interesting character, try a young Camembert (cow milk, France). The emerging vegetal aromas and flavor in the cheese will add depth to the wine's flavor. A Cheddar-style cheese such as Cabot Clothbound Cheddar (cow milk, United States) shows yogurty notes and hints of sweet hay, delicious with Gamay. Slightly aged goat milk cheeses are also great matches for this young wine. Try a Blue Ledge Farm Crottina (goat milk, United States).

MATCH MADE IN HEAVEN

One of Beaujolais's greatest friends in the culinary world is charcuterie, especially saucisson (French salami). Try a gently chilled Cru Beaujolais from the village of Morgon with the ancient Cantal cheese (cow milk, France) and a few slices of Rosette de Lyon, a red wine and garlic saucisson.

FACT

In 1395, the Duke of Burgundy, Philippe the Bold, outlawed the Gamay grape in favor of the more elegant Pinot Noir, deeming Gamay too harsh for general consumption. Sixty years later, Philippe the Good only made it worse by reinforcing the ban, stating, "The Dukes of Burgundy are known as the lords of the best wines in Christendom. We will maintain our reputation!"

GRENACHE/GARNACHA

Grenache (in French), or Garnacha (in Spanish), was once thought to have originated in Sardinia, Italy. Recent evidence, however, suggests Spain may be where it all started. Regardless, it is widely planted in southern France, Spain, and Italy, and is often used as a blending grape.

THE WINE

Spanish origins make total sense for this wine—Grenache's spicy and peppery notes pair perfectly with Spanish cuisine. In southern France, it is often mixed with Syrah and Mourvèdre to form the classic Rhône blend nicknamed "GSM" for each grape's initials. These wines show deep notes of spicy red fruits, especially raspberry. Because it is mostly grown in hot climates, these wines typically have high alcohol while keeping acidity and tannins to a milder level.

THE CHEESE THAT LOVES IT

Grenache is best when paired with mild cheeses that have enough body to "support" the wine's weight on the tongue. A favorite pairing is Gouda on the older side. Try Veenweidekaas Reserve (cow milk, The Netherlands). The two-plus years of aging mellows out the cheese, putting it in harmony with the wine's gentle tannins. Also, try the always interesting Red Leicester (cow milk, England), ideally one that is aged for six months or so to develop the tangy notes that work so well here.

MATCH MADE IN HEAVEN

Spanish Garnacha with El Chamizo (cow and sheep milk, Spain), a cheese made in the style of Manchego, but with pimentón rubbed on the rind to give it a gorgeous, mottled appearance. Alongside, serve black cherry preserves that have just a touch of pimente d'Espelette mixed in (a traditional Basque chile pepper used in cooking). The slight bite of the pepper complements the spice in the wine, and the dark fruit notes in both the wine and the preserves are a fantastic counterpoint to the body of the cheese.

FACT

Despite being one of the world's most planted grape varietals, Grenache has little presence in the new world except for in Australia and California. As its popularity spreads, new vines are being planted in unusual spots such as Mexico, Uruguay, and Chile.

MERLOT

Thanks in part to bad cinematic treatment recently, Merlot's reputation has taken a bit of a wholly undeserved shot. For shame! This amazing grape is second only to its best friend, Cabernet Sauvignon, in worldwide production. Open a bottle and see what all the fuss isn't about.

THE WINE

Merlots are valued not only for their plummy, jammy notes and soft tannins, but also for their textural feel. Merlots are often described as "smooth" and "round," both sensations, rather than tastes or flavors. Unlike many other wine grapes, Merlot grapes have an unusually large body relative to their seeds (called "pips") and skin thickness. This yields a juice that ferments into a velvety-smooth wine. It is often blended with Cabernet Sauvignon, especially in Bordeaux, where it is the top-planted grape of all.

THE CHEESE THAT LOVES IT

The smoothness of the wine, the soft tannins, and the deep fruit notes make Merlot a great choice for cheeses that have full-bodied flavor. Try the supple and aromatic Livarot (cow milk, France) or a mild and creamy Paglierina (cow and sheep milk, Italy). The wine's soft tannins go well with the cheese's equally soft texture. For a bolder pairing, try an aged Pecorino di Pienza Morchiato (sheep milk, Italy) or Gruyère Vieux (cow milk, Switzerland).

MATCH MADE IN HEAVEN

Merlot with Brebis Abbaye de Belloc (sheep milk, France) and some pruneaux d'Agen—dried Ente plums from the Aquitaine region of southwestern France. The full-bodied Brebis has a big mouthfeel and a mildly sweet, nutty note that is almost caramelly. The wine's soft tannins add to the luxuriousness of the combination, and the prunes bring out plum notes in the wine while being as soft and rich as the cheese and wine. A spectacular combination—and one of my all-time favorites.

FACT

Thanks to a memorable scene in the 2004 movie *Sideways*, people have long asserted the movie's impact on Merlot and Pinot Noir sales (in the scene the lead character, a Pinot Noir fan, rails against Merlot, adamantly refusing to drink it), creating what is known as the "*Sideways* Effect." Research concluded that though the movie did increase the volume of Pinot Noir consumed, it didn't damage Merlot's reputation anywhere near what people think.

PINOT NOIR

More than any other wine grape in the world, Pinot Noir is at once lauded for its magnificence and cursed for its difficulty. It is the top grape in Burgundy, France, where it makes some of the most expressive and perfumed red wines in the entire world, and it is grown all over the winemaking globe. Those who love Pinot Noir do so almost to a point of obsession.

THE WINE

Pinots from old-world producers really exhibit terroir. Old-world Pinots have aromas of red fruit like cherry or strawberry, as well as earthy tones and often mushroomy or meaty aromas as well. New-world wines show more fruit and often have a jamlike aroma to them. Softer tannins and a silky texture are found in both styles. When made well, any Pinot Noir has the potential to be one of the most enjoyable bottles you'll ever have.

THE CHEESE THAT LOVES IT

New-world Pinot Noir (from Chile, for example) enjoys pairing with a simple, soft complexion. Try Jasper Hill's bloomy-rinded Moses Sleeper (cow milk, United States) or a slightly aged goat milk cheese such as Chevrot (France). Old-world wines (especially those from Burgundy, the home of Pinot Noir) pair well with cheeses that are a bit more aromatic. Try a middle-aged Camembert (cow milk, France) or a washed-rind L'Ami du Chambertin (cow milk, France).

MATCH MADE IN HEAVEN

There is a saying—what grows together goes together. This logic is spot-on when you pair a Pinot Noir from Burgundy with Époisses de Bourgogne, a cow milk cheese washed in marc (locally made pomace brandy) as it ages. This washing gives the cheese its distinctive orange rind and pungent odor. The interior of the cheese is soft and luxurious. To emphasize the wine's red fruit characteristics, serve this with dried cherries or a dollop of cherry jam.

FACT

Recent DNA testing proved what was suspected for a while now, which is that almost all of the world's pinots are related. The two most popular white pinots, Pinot Grigio and Pinot Blanc, are actually mutations of Pinot Noir. They simply have color mutations. Another fun fact: Pinot Noir predates Cabernet Sauvignon by more than a thousand years!

ZWEIGELT

The most widely planted red grape in Austria is only now gaining ground in the American wine consciousness. A crossing of St. Laurent and Blaufränkisch, Zweigelt is named for the man who created it in 1922. Ranging in style from simple and fruity to complex and age-worthy, it is becoming known among more casual wine lovers.

THE WINE

The majority of Zweigelt found in the United States are dry wines. Few of the sweet, dessert-style wines make it out of Austria, although Canada does make a small selection. Zweigelt takes the best characteristics from each of the parent grapes. The Blaufränkisch genes lend spiciness and crisp acidity. From St. Laurent come the bright cherry notes that are often mistaken for Pinot Noir, especially when Zweigelt is aged a bit, emphasizing the silkiness that can result from it.

THE CHEESE THAT LOVES IT

The bright fruit notes and hint of spice make Zweigelt a versatile cheese wine. To emphasize the fun fruit notes and acidity, select a mild, semisoft cheese that won't challenge the wine too much. Try Saint-Nectaire (cow milk, France) or fontina (cow milk, Italy). Both cheeses are mild and have simple milky, salty flavors, which allow the wine's zippy red fruit notes to shine through. For a more complex pairing, select a pressed-curd cheese (Cheddar is the most well-known example). Try Laguiole (cow milk, France) or Lincolnshire Poacher (cow milk, England). The firm, cakey texture and sharp bite of these cheeses match well with the tang of the wine, especially in the finish.

MATCH MADE IN HEAVEN

Monte Veronese Latte Intero (cow milk, Italy) and fresh raspberries. This cheese is as "Italian table cheese" as it gets. Made in the northeastern Veneto region of Italy, Latte Intero has a semisoft, pliant interior that is sweetly milky and finishes cleanly with a slight tang that complements Zweigelt's spicy notes. The fresh raspberries add a lively, fruity flavor that makes the berry notes of the wine really punch out. The natural acidity of the fruit keeps the combination crisp and fun.

PAIRING MEDIUM-TO HEAVY-TANNIN RED WINES WITH CHEESE

For many people, light and fruity red wine simply won't do. They need wine with intensity and bold flavors. Usually, they're looking for a wine with higher levels of tannins, giving the wine bigger structure and more horsepower. Accordingly, the best cheeses to pair with these wines are just as intense and bold. Aged cheeses usually work well because aging intensifies their flavor and assertiveness. More tannic red wines also pair nicely with washed-rind cheeses. These cheeses have liquid applied to them as they age (often brine, but many other options are available, including wine, beer, spirits, and honey). The result is a cheese that is funky and aromatic on the outside, but creamy and nuanced on the inside. Finally, consider pairing these red wines with blue cheeses. The bluing gives the cheese stronger, more energetic flavors and textures, which are perfect with the increased tannins.

CHILL OR NOT TO CHILL?

Contrary to popular belief, red wine can be served chilled! Chilling a beverage increases the refreshment factor, but can make individual flavors more difficult to perceive because fewer aromatic molecules are dancing around (they're too cold). Some restaurants now offer diners the option of enjoying a red wine served chilled with their appetizers, and the same bottle is then enjoyed throughout the meal. As additional courses are served, the wine continues to warm to the perfect temperature for each part of the meal.

TEMPRANILLO

At the heart of almost every great wine from Spain and Portugal lurks Tempranillo, which is now used successfully in new-world locales such as Argentina and the United States, particularly California. This thick-skinned grape yields wines that are dark and bold, yet softer than you might expect.

THE WINE

The Tempranillo grape tends to develop less acid than other hot-weather grapes. Because of this, these wines are still lively and fresh tasting, but have a mellowness and warmth to them that is quite appealing. Some Tempranillos can have more pronounced tannins, and the occasional wine will have strong tannins. Tempranillo has elegant aromas of dried strawberries, tobacco leaves, and vanilla. Flavors of plum, dark red fruits, and vanilla from oak aging make Tempranillo a fantastic companion for many foods, especially cheese.

THE CHEESE THAT LOVES IT

The bold flavors and full aromas of Tempranillo are best suited with cheeses that can match the wine's intensity. Texture isn't quite as much an issue here, but semisoft to hard cheeses will work best. Try a moderately aged Serra da Estrela (sheep milk, Portugal). The springy to firm texture and pungent horsepower from washing the rind is more than up to the task of handling the wine's assertiveness. Also try Tomme de Savoie (cow milk, France), the classic cheese from the French Alps. The earthy, natural rind and milky interior play well with the medium tannins in the wine.

MATCH MADE IN HEAVEN

Serve a Tempranillo with a well-aged Manchego, the classic sheep milk cheese from Spain. The animal bite and saltiness of the aged sheep milk complement the wine's strength well. Black cherry preserves are a natural here (cherries and sheep milk cheeses are best pals). For a more authentic Spanish experience, serve this combination with membrillo, a thick and sweet quince paste and salty Marcona almonds.

FACT

Unlike many other varietals used to make red wine, Tempranillo has a rather mild and mellow aroma and relatively neutral flavor. These characteristics make it popular with winemakers because it allows them to impart their own nuances and styles into the wines more readily than if the grape was bringing its own, stronger characteristics to the party.

CABERNET SAUVIGNON

Arguably the most popular red wine grape on the planet, Cabernet Sauvignon is a highly adaptable vine and is grown in virtually every winemaking region in the world. Recent DNA testing confirmed this grape is the genetic offspring of a crossing between Cabernet Franc and Sauvignon Blanc. A vigorous grower, this grape tends to mature slowly, allowing the winemaker to get the most character possible from it when harvested.

THE WINE

Even though it is grown pretty much everywhere, all Cabernet Sauvignons share characteristics of deep color and structure, not too much acidity, and aromas of spices, dark berries, and cedar wood. Most old-world producers use Cabernet Sauvignon as a blending grape (especially Bordeaux, where it is blended with Merlot). For producers who do make a single-variety wine from it, it's common to smell aromas of violets, licorice, black cherry, earth, and even leather and tobacco—very "suit-and-tie" sort of stuff. New-world Cabernet Sauvignons are usually higher in alcohol from growing in hotter weather. They tend to have a little bit of a black pepper aroma mixed in with the black cherry and licorice notes. New-world Cabernet Sauvignons usually have softer tannins.

THE CHEESE THAT LOVES IT

The peppery notes and big mouthfeel allow this wine to stand up to some pretty powerful cheeses. For a bold combination, pair an old-world wine with Stilton (cow milk, England), one of the kings of the blue cheese world. The silky texture and salty, animal flavor of the cheese works delightfully with the wine's tannins, leaving a soft and fruity finish on the palate. New-world Cabernet Sauvignons pair well with medium-bodied cheeses such as Cheddar and medium-aged Comté. These cheeses' rich texture and notes of toasted nuts and caramel bring out the vanilla notes in the wine.

MATCH MADE IN HEAVEN

Cabernet Sauvignon's dark cherry aromas and full tannins make it a winner with sheep milk cheeses—try Pecorino Gran Riserva, an aged sheep milk cheese from Tuscany, and one of the finest pecorinos in the world. Add a daub of blackberry jam to round out the pairing. The jam emphasizes the black fruit notes of the wine and the sugars add a fullness to the texture. A very luxurious pairing.

MALBEC

This dark-skinned grape, originally known as Côt, originated in southern France, where it was often used for blending. The best expressions of this wine unquestionably come from Argentina, where it was brought by a French botanist in the mid-nineteenth century.

THE WINE

Because the Malbec grape is sensitive to growing conditions, ripeness plays an important part in outcome. Thinner-skinned grapes yield wines that are fruitier and softer. Thicker-skinned grapes allow for wines that are more concentrated and intense in body and flavor. All Malbecs tend to be deeply colored, with some even looking inky black. Aromas of black fruits and a touch of game meats complement the flavors of plums and blackberries. French Malbecs will have red fruit notes like cherry and sometimes raspberry, and Argentinean wines favor darker black fruit notes. Argentinean Malbecs may also have an earthy aroma, flavors of dark chocolate, and bright acidity.

THE CHEESE THAT LOVES IT

French Malbec can pair well with cheeses that have a little horsepower to them. For a softer-textured cheese, try Caciotta Toscana (cow and sheep milk, Italy) with a French Malbec. The wine's leathery aroma and slight bitterness counter the cheese's fatty texture and flavor, while the tannins cut through the soft, supple interior quite nicely. Harder cheeses like Terrincho Velho (sheep milk, Portugal) have the backbone to handle the wine's strength. Malbec is also a good partner for blue cheeses that have farmy notes. Try Cashel Blue (cow milk, Ireland). The cheese has a touch of farminess that counters the wine's fruity acidity well, and the minerally finish pleasantly rivals the wine.

MATCH MADE IN HEAVEN

Manchego Curado (sheep milk, Spain), with its bold flavor and texture from aging for approximately six months, is a great partner for the wine. Each lends its own strength and character to the pairing without getting lost. The cheese's saltiness softens the tannins in the wine and "rounds the edges" a bit. For a classic Manchego pairing, serve this with membrillo, a sweet and thick quince paste. To emphasize the dark fruit notes of the wine, serve fresh blackberries when in season. An unusual and amazing pairing is Manchego, Malbec, and a chunk of top-notch dark chocolate. When made well, dark chocolate often exhibits flavors of blueberry and similar dark berries. It's subtle enough that it doesn't distract, and it adds a rich, deep tone to the combination.

NEBBIOLO

One of the most revered and lauded Italian wine grapes, Nebbiolo is the engine of Barolo and Barbaresco, whose core notes of "tar and roses" entice wine lovers the world over. Nebbiolo wines tend to lose their color rather quickly by red wine standards— often a couple of years of aging yields a wine much lighter in color than might be expected. Because of the value of the grape and subsequent wines, Nebbiolo grapes enjoy the best plots of land and some of the greatest care and handling in all of Italy.

THE WINE

Nebbiolo is a fussy grape that yields wines that are powerful and intense, with aromas and flavors that include tobacco, dried cherries, violets, roses, and truffles. More than almost any other grape, Nebbiolo really benefits from aging, especially when it takes the prestigious form of Barolo. Barbaresco, another powerhouse red made from the same grape, tends to be slightly softer and more perfumed. These wines tend to not be very fruity or playful. They are austere and magnificent!

THE CHEESE THAT LOVES IT

Nebbiolo benefits from a cheese that is as serious as the wine is. The best bet is a hard, aged cheese like a three-year Parmigiano-Reggiano Riserva (cow milk, Italy). The bolder, rustic notes of the cheese pair well with the wine's hearty flavors and aromas.

MATCH MADE IN HEAVEN

Pair a well-aged Nebbiolo (Barolo, if the wallet will cooperate) with a cheese that features truffles, such as Sottocenere al Tartufo (cow milk, Italy). The cheese has a semi-firm, pleasing texture and is studded with black truffles. Each bite releases the delicate aromas and flavors of the truffles, which augment the wine's savory qualities. This is a very sophisticated combination.

FACT

Sottocenere ("under ash" in Italian) is originally from Venice and made with raw cow milk and slices of truffle. The ash was originally used to preserve and protect the wheel until it matured enough and could be handled.

PINOTAGE

*South Africa's very own grape was created in 1925 in Stellenbosch, the result of combining Pinot Noir and Cinsault. The name **Pinotage** comes from a portmanteau of the parent grapes, with the nobler Pinot coming first. Outside of South Africa, a little Pinotage is grown in New Zealand, but hardly anywhere else.*

THE WINE

The quality of Pinotage hinges on the quality of the grapes harvested. A bad Pinotage can be over-acidic and over-tannic, a recipe for disaster. When made well, the wine takes the perfumed majesty of Pinot Noir and combines it with the earthy, lively power of the Cinsault grape. Aromas of plums and berry abound, with the occasional hint of coffee beans and earth. Pinotage flavors of dark berries, earth, and plums are most common, with some better-made wines having a smoky quality as well. When purchasing Pinotage, spending a little bit more for a better bottle usually pays off.

THE CHEESE THAT LOVES IT

The bigger the cheese, the better. Pinotage brings a lot of intensity to the pairing, and the cheese better be able to handle it. Aged grana cheeses work well here. Try a three-year Parmigiano-Reggiano (cow milk, Italy) or Grana Padano (cow milk, Italy). The intensity from aging lets the cheese keep pace with the tannic wine. If the Pinotage is particularly smoky, an aged Gouda would emphasize that quality. If you are drinking a milder Pinotage, try Vacherin Fribourgeois (cow milk, Switzerland). The nuttiness and texture of the cheese readily handle the wine's attitude.

MATCH MADE IN HEAVEN

A well-made Pinotage and Sbrinz (cow milk, Switzerland). Thought to be Europe's oldest cheese, Sbrinz is a very hard cheese, often aged for two to three years. It is spicy and aromatic, with a long finish. Both the wine and the cheese are power-houses, and big, large flavors come from bringing them together. There aren't too many condiments that stand a chance alongside these two monsters, but charcuterie that has a rich, smoky note would be your best shot. Smoked meats such as Italian speck or even smoked bacon would fit in well here.

PRIMITIVO

Better known as Zinfandel in California, Primitivo is the Italian designation for the Croatian grape Tribidrag. Named "first to ripen" in Latin (primativus), Primitivo is most commonly found in Apulia, the Italian "heel of the boot."

THE WINE

Primitivo grows up in the hot, arid climate of southern Italy. As a result, most of the wines are high in alcohol and tannins, making them anything but timid and mellow. If you're looking for a wine to match your four-alarm chili or spicy barbecue, Primitivo is your guy. The aroma is thick and full, with hints of dried cherries and spiced berries. The high alcohol makes this wine taste hot and strong, so make sure the foods served with Primitivo have a similar attitude problem—spicy, meaty foods work best.

THE CHEESE THAT LOVES IT

Primitivo calls for bold flavors. Blue cheeses work well because they keep pace with the wine's brute strength. Try Gorgonzola naturale (cow milk, Italy). The cheese's piquant aromas and strong bluing make a great partner to the wine's hot alcohol note. Aged, hard cheeses also handle the wine. Try Asiago Stravecchio (cow milk, Italy), a cheese reminiscent of Parmigiano-Reggiano that is aged for at least eighteen months. The intense flavor of the cheese will match the wine.

MATCH MADE IN HEAVEN

Primitivo with MitiBleu (sheep milk, Spain). This uncommon cheese is made in the style of Roquefort, but with less minerality. The dark flavors pair well with the wine's equally dark characteristics. MitiBleu's saltiness mixes with Primitivo's tannins, resulting in a soft, opulent mouth-feel that is velvety and pleasing. Each part of this combination is assertive and forward—bringing them together keeps both in check!

FACT

In 2003, a Spanish entrepreneur saw an opportunity to produce a blue cheese designed to rival one of the kings of the blue cheese world—France's noble Roquefort—using raw ewe's milk (as Roquefort does) to make wheels that are similar in size and texture. Aged for four months, Mitibleu is spicy and pungent, but with lower acidity than Roquefort, making the mouthfeel a bit softer and less aggressive.

SANGIOVESE

Best known as the grape in Chianti, Sangiovese is critical to the success of the Italian wine industry. It is one of the most widely planted grapes in all of Italy. Because of that proliferation, Sangiovese goes by many different names in many different places. Fortunately, all these places still yield a wine that is lightly colored, medium to heavily tannic, and highly acidic.

THE WINE

Bright fruit flavors, firm tannins, and excellent balance are Sangiovese's calling card. Because it is so widely planted, many style variations may be found. Generally, aromas of black and red fruits, and sometimes flowers are common. Sangiovese's flavors include wild strawberry, blackberry, sour cherry, and often subtle orange peel. Some versions may show an herbal flavor as well, although less commonly.

THE CHEESE THAT LOVES IT

Cheeses with some body but not too strong a flavor are great. Try a young pecorino (sheep milk, Italy), one that is still soft and pliable. The supple cheese is contrasted by the wine's acidity and tannins for a fun flavor combination. Young Crescenza (cow milk, Italy) and alpine-style cheeses also work well. Try Spring Brook Tarentaise (cow milk, United States). Semisoft, mild cheeses let the wine's body and tannins do the heavy lifting in the pairing—try a soft provolone (cow milk, Italy) or Monte Veronese Latte Intero (cow milk, Italy).

MATCH MADE IN HEAVEN

Chianti with Parmigiano-Reggiano (cow milk, Italy) and sour cherry preserves. The wine's brightness melds nicely with the preserve's tanginess. The cheese is salty and full-bodied, providing the perfect canvas for the cherry notes of the wine and condiment to shine.

FACT

It is thought the name of the grape derives from sanguis Jove, the "blood of Jove," the old Italian name for Jupiter, the Roman king of the gods and the god of sky and thunder, leading most to believe Sangiovese originated in Tuscany. Recent research suggests it may have migrated from southern Italy and melded with the northern grape Ciliegiolo, making it half-Tuscan and half-Calabrese.

SYRAH/SHIRAZ

Although these two wines come from the genetically identical Syrah grape, there are significant stylistic differences between them, enough for the wine world to consider them distinct varieties. Both are full-bodied and deeply colored wines that work well with food.

THE WINE

In France, Syrah is at home in the northern Rhône, where it is peppery and earthy, sometimes even a bit smoky, with licorice and dark berry flavors. French Syrah is appreciated for its aging potential, which in some wines can top ten years. Shiraz, the Australian version, shares the dark berry and spicy aromas and flavors of its European doppelganger, but adds secondary flavors of chocolate and blueberry. The Aussie wines also tend to be "jammy," with a rich, coating mouthfeel.

THE CHEESE THAT LOVES IT

Syrah and Shiraz can be a little difficult to pair with cheeses because of their strength and intensity. Cheeses with body and a little aging work well. Try Edam (cow milk, The Netherlands) or an aged Gouda. Cheddar can work well, particularly sharp Cheddar. For pairing with a softer cheese, try Saint-Nectaire (cow milk, France), a semisoft cheese from the Auvergne that has character and a soft texture similar to the classic French cheese Reblochon.

MATCH MADE IN HEAVEN

Australian Shiraz with the classic English blue cheese Stilton and a daub of blueberry jam. The cheese is strong and complex enough to equal the wine's intensity. The blueberry jam brings out the dark fruit jam characteristic of the Shiraz. Delicious!

FACT

Australian 'Shiraz' is varietally the same grape as French (and elsewhere) Syrah. When it was first introduced to the Land Down Under in 1832, a name was needed to differentiate the distinctly different style of wine being made. It was decided to name their wines after the Iranian city from which the Syrah grape was thought to have been first grown, Shiraz.

PETITE SIRAH

Also known as Durif (named for the grape's creator), this intensely colored little grape packs quite a punch with high acidity and tannins, giving this wine excellent aging potential. It was created in the late nineteenth century and is a direct descendant of French Syrah.

THE WINE

Blackberry, dark chocolate, and blueberry are common flavors found in Petite Sirah, along with licorice and sometimes black pepper. These are full-bodied and deeply colored wines.

THE CHEESE THAT LOVES IT

The strength and power of the wine works well with cheeses that can match its intensity. Aged cheeses such as Mahon (cow milk, Spain) or Pecorino Gran Riserva (sheep milk, Italy) will keep pace with the intensity the wine brings. Sheep milk cheeses will also work well because their higher fat content will smooth out the wine's tannins nicely. Try Berkswell (Great Britain) or Zamorano (Spain).

MATCH MADE IN HEAVEN

Brebis du Haut-Béarn (sheep milk, France) with blackcurrant preserves. The dark berry notes of the jam match those in the wine, while the opulent mouthfeel of the cheese is perfectly cut by the high tannins in the wine.

FACT

The "petit" in this grape's name refers to the berry size, certainly not its flavor. Because of the grape's diminutive size, the ratio of skin to juice is high. This means extended maceration (the leaching of tannins and colorants from grape skins) can yield a highly tannic wine if the winemaker isn't careful.

ZINFANDEL

The American twin to Italian Primitivo, "Zin" came to the States in the mid-nineteenth century from Europe. It landed in California, especially Lodi and Sonoma, where it continues to thrive.

THE WINE

Zinfandel is powerful and assertive. Because it grows in the hot California sun, Zinfandel is high in alcohol, often exceeding 14 percent alcohol by volume. Deeply colored and full-bodied, Zinfandel usually shows aromas of red berries and dried herbs, and may smell "hot" from the alcohol content. Zinfandel has flavors of raspberry, spice, and bramble.

THE CHEESE THAT LOVES IT

Zinfandel is best with cheeses that are assertive and even a bit salty. Try Raclette (cow milk, Switzerland). The intense flavors and saltiness of the cheese bring out the fruit notes in the wine. From Sicily, Canestrato (a blend of sheep and goat milks) goes nicely with the tannins and hot characteristic of the wine. A savory Gruyère Vieux (cow milk, Switzerland) will provide enough backbone and add a pleasing nuttiness to the combination.

MATCH MADE IN HEAVEN

California old-vine Zinfandel with Italian Asiago (cow milk) and fresh Bing cherries. The bright fruit flavors of the cherries and the wine are perfect complements to the saltiness of the cheese. Asiago's nutty and sweet flavors are balanced by a slight sharpness on the finish, which matches Zinfandel's spicy and lingering finish quite nicely.

FACT

Both Zinfandel and its Italian counterpart Primitivo are genetically identical to the Croatian grapes Crljenak and Tribidrag. Research suggests these grapes have been grown in Croatia for thousands of years. The grape we know as Zinfandel first shows up in Long Island, New York, around 1829. Shortly thereafter, a Bostonian named Samuel Perkins started selling "Zenfendal." It was brought to California in the 1850s during the gold rush, where it took hold and thrived.

A NOTE ON ROSÉ WINES

Recent years have seen a resurgence of Americans enjoying rosé wines, and that is great to see. For too long, "rosé" meant cheaply made, pink-tinted sweet wines that were closer to fruit punch than the magnificently dry yet fruity wines being enjoyed elsewhere in the world.

The concept of rosé wines is simple—they combine the best aspects of white and red wines. They are best served chilled like white wines for maximum refreshment, but have more body and structure like red wines, which makes them excellent for food pairings. The "rosé" in rosé wines comes from the red grape skins soaking in the fermenting wine for a short time. When making red wine, the skins are left in with the grape juice. Heat from the fermentation causes the pigments in the skin to bleed into the wine and stain it red. The longer the contact and darker the skin to begin with, the darker the wine. Leave the red grape skin in for a short time and, voilà! You have rosé wine.

America's rekindled love of rosé wines is fantastic, especially for food lovers. More attention by wine consumers means better wines are being sent our way. Few wines have the broad food pairing appeal of rosé wines.

PAIRING ROSÉ WINES WITH CHEESE

The main consideration when pairing cheese with these wines is how fruity and dry the wine is, because that determines the kind of cheese that will work best. Rosé wines can range from salmon-pink and smelling of grapefruit to deep red with aromas of black cherries. Generally speaking, the darker the wine, the deeper the flavor.

LIGHT- TO MEDIUM-BODIED ROSÉ WINES AND THE CHEESES THAT LOVE THEM

Lighter rosé wines typically have aromas of light fruits like strawberries and grapefruit. They tend to be very dry, with a gentle mouthfeel and bright, vivid acidity. For these wines, use cheeses that have bright, tangy flavors to match the wine's liveliness. Consider a fresh goat cheese like Pouligny Saint Pierre (goat milk, France). This pyramid-shaped cheese has an interesting balance of sweet milk and hay aromas, with flavors that are a touch sour and sweet themselves. The energy of a rosé matches the personality of the cheese quite well. Another choice might be a mild cow milk cheese with a soft interior. Try Scimudin (cow milk, Italy), a bloomy-rinded cheese that is soft on the inside and has a mild, almost sweet flavor. The fresh berry flavors of the rosé will contrast the milky flavor and texture beautifully. For a condiment, try a rosehip preserve. The delicate rose notes of the preserve marry the wine and cheese.

FULL-BODIED ROSÉ WINES AND THE CHEESES THAT LOVE THEM

Rosé wines made from bolder grapes like Malbec have a deeper color, with stronger aromas and flavors of cherry and raspberry. Their bigger personality means they can handle bigger cheeses, relatively speaking. Instead of fresh goat cheeses and soft cow milk cheeses, these wines pair well with young Gruyères (cow milk, Switzerland), as well as most Brebis (sheep milk) from the Pyrénées in France. The richer tones and fuller body of the cheeses are great companions to the wine's fuller fruit notes. To emphasize the fruitiness, add a spoonful of strawberry preserves or some dried berries.

(6)

DESSERT AND FORTIFIED WINES

Most wine-producing countries in the world make a dessert wine, a fortified wine, or both. France has Sauternes and Vin Doux. Italy makes Vin Santo. Spain has sweet sherry. Portugal has port. The list goes on and on. It's hardly surprising—the rich, opulent flavors and textures of a well-crafted dessert or fortified wine are immensely satisfying. And who doesn't like flavors of vanilla and butterscotch, apricots and honey, or sweet red berries? Not only are these wines the perfect conclusion to a decadent meal or a delicious way to ward off the cold on a chilly winter night, they are also amazingly adept at pairing with bold cheeses, creating some of the most striking combinations you'll ever experience.

Often grouped together, these two kinds of wines are actually quite different. The end result is the same—sweet, viscous wine with big flavors and high alcohol, right? Not quite. Unlike fortified wines, dessert wines are always sweet, with lots of sugar and no added alcohol. Unlike dessert wines, fortified wines can be made sweet or dry. The name "fortified" has more to do with the method of producing and stabilizing the wines than with sweetening them. Understanding the basic differences between them goes a long way toward making the best choice for your cheese plate.

THE BASICS OF DESSERT AND FORTIFIED WINES

Dessert wines are made with higher levels of sugar and usually an accompanying level of alcohol. Some dessert wines achieve this from allowing grapes to naturally develop higher levels of sugar during the season. Some achieve this by allowing the grapes to freeze in the cold weather, causing the grape to lose moisture but keep the sugar. Some even allow certain kinds of mold to form on the surface of the grapes, causing the grapes to lose water while retaining the sugar. These wines are made in such a way these higher sugars are kept, creating a wine that is virtually a dessert in itself.

With fortified wines, the process is different. Long before modern, reliable techniques existed to protect wines from spoilage, a discovery was made. Adding alcohol (usually brandy) to wine helped protect it by "fortifying" it, raising the alcohol level high enough that bacterial spoilage couldn't occur. An unintentional side effect of this was the halting of any fermentation. That meant any remaining sugar wasn't turned into alcohol. The remaining sugar made the wine sweet, and the addition of alcohol made it even boozier. In other cases, like sherry, there are varying degrees of sweetness or dryness, depending on the style of the wine being made. The range is broad, and the differences pronounced. They all have one thing in common—the ability to create spectacular wine and cheese pairings.

PAIRING WITH CHEESE

The biggest factor to remember when pairing dessert and fortified wines with cheese is these wines themselves may be bigger, more flavorful, and at times bolder than many cheeses. That doesn't mean they can't be used for pairings, but the cheeses that accompany them need to be just as assertive. Consider the wine and its characteristics. Is it a sweet and thick dessert wine? Then be sure to pair it with a cheese that is also big and full-flavored. Is the wine dry, with a bit of sea air aroma (like some sherries)? Then consider a cheese with more age on it that may also taste a bit saltier than a younger cheese.

Another consideration for these pairings is whether or not a condiment will be involved. The additional flavor or texture it brings can change the overall character of the pairing, sometimes quite significantly. In the next chapter, condiments and their place in pairings are discussed. For now, just keep in mind their ability to help shape the pairing. Salted almonds may help bring out the saline quality of a fino sherry, and dried figs will really emphasize the rich, sweet characteristics of a tawny port. Let's look at some specific examples.

BRACHETTO

One of northern Italy's favorite party sippers, this wine is thought to have first been identified in the late nineteenth century. It was originally made as a dry wine, but almost all versions made after 1970 are the sweet and frothy wine loved today. Brachetto is often thought of as Moscato's "red sibling."

THE WINE

Fruity, fizzy, and fun, Brachetto is made from the eponymous grape and is at its best in Piedmont, Italy. Fermentation takes place in pressurized tanks, giving the wine pep and energy. This wine is highly aromatic, smelling of roses, raspberries, and other red fruits. The flavor is sweet and loaded with berries, but surprisingly refreshing. Because Brachetto is low in alcohol, it can be enjoyed sip after sip after sip! Be sure to serve this wine cold.

THE CHEESE THAT LOVES IT

Pairing cheese with this wine is all about enjoying the opulent textures and richness the wine brings. Cheeses that match Brachetto's simple, opulent fun are best. Soft and creamy interior cheeses like Brebirousse d'Argental (sheep milk, France) have the chewy, melt-in-your-mouth texture that pairs so well with the body of the wine. For a bolder experience, pair Brachetto with a full-bodied blue cheese like Gorgonzola dolce (cow milk, Italy). This cheese has a higher fat content than the Gorgonzola naturale, and matches the wine's body for a satisfying combination. Cheeses with a high salt content may work well, as the "sweet and salty" combination is usually pleasant.

MATCH MADE IN HEAVEN

Brillat-Savarin (cow milk, France) with fresh raspberries. This addictive triple-crème cheese is all about pleasure. The almost spreadable interior is sweetly creamy in flavor, with just a hint of salt. The sweet body of the wine is right at home, matching the cheese's full, rich body. The fresh raspberries are the real magic here, though. Their natural sugars pair nicely with the wine, while their bright flavor cuts through the weight of the wine and cheese. If possible, serve the berries chilled to turn up the refreshment factor.

FACT

Originally thought to be the same as the French grape Braquet, recent research has disproved that theory. It is now thought this tasty little fellow originated in the hills of Monferrato, as it first mentioned in writings from there in 1877.

ICE WINE

A generic name for sweet dessert wines made from grapes frozen on the vine to concentrate the sugars in them, ice wines are made where the weather gets cold enough to create those circumstances. Ice wines are usually sold in half bottles because of their sweetness and strength. A few sips is usually more than enough for the wine enthusiast's sweet tooth.

THE WINE

Ice wines are commonly made from Riesling or Vidal grapes because they are well suited to cold climates and make lots of sugar, although many new-world producers are experimenting with more common grapes like Merlot, Cabernet Sauvignon, and Chardonnay. Generally, all ice wines have a thick, viscous body and are extremely aromatic, with sweet aromas of white flowers, mangoes, and other tropical fruits. Even though the body is heavy and coating, a well-made ice wine will actually be quite refreshing because of the high amount of acidity that keeps it bright and sharp, with flavors of honey, apricots, and similar white fruits.

THE CHEESE THAT LOVES IT

Ice wines want a dance partner that is as big and round as it is. Cheeses that have a high fat content work really well because the cheese's big textures match the wine. Try the whipped cream–like mascarpone (cow milk, Italy). The cheese's thick yet airy texture is more than up for the task of handling the wine's heft. Blue cheeses are another excellent choice because the sweet viscosity and high alcohol of the wine mellow all but the most savage blues into nutty, tangy combinations. Try North Country Blue (cow milk, United States), a pungent and forward blue cheese that is fantastically suited to the wine's sweetness.

MATCH MADE IN HEAVEN

Bleu des Basques (sheep milk, France) with fresh nectarines. This blue cheese is milky sweet, with an incredible flavor that is clean and sharp. This pairing is all about complementing the richness of the wine with the equally hedonistic body of the cheese. The nectarines add a bright fruit flavor and the natural fruit acidity peps everything up a touch.

FACT

Meaning "blue from the Basque region," Bleu des Basques is a fantastic representation of the full-bodied and robust cheeses enjoyed in the French Basque region, where sheep milk cheeses are common. Often they are mixed with the locally-grown pimente d'Espelette, a chili pepper that finds its way into all aspects of Basque cooking.

MADEIRA

Named for the Portuguese islands where it is made, this fortified wine is often overlooked because cheap versions are used in cooking. When made well, Madeira wines are elegant and a great choice for pairing with a wide variety of foods, especially cheese.

THE WINE

Madeira comes in four major styles. Sercial is bright and dry with almond aromas and flavors. Verdelho is slightly darker with more smoky aromas but is still dry. Bual is darker still, with some sweetness, and usually has a raisiny flavor. Malvasia (also known as Malmsey) is the darkest and sweetest of the four styles, with a heavier body and flavors of coffee and caramel. Because the grapes used in making Madeira have a high level of acidity, the wines keep a bright, refreshing quality to them, making them fantastic pairing wines for cheeses. Generally, Madeira wines have more acidity and brightness to them than port wines do.

THE CHEESE THAT LOVES IT

As with pretty much all dessert wines, blue cheeses are a great match. The cheese's bite offsets the wine's sweetness and density. Try the formidable Queso Azul de Valdeon (cow and goat milk, Spain) with the full-throttle sweetness of a Malvasia Madeira. For a subtler pairing, enhance a Verdelho Madeira's nutty smokiness with an equally nutty cheese like Appenzeller (cow milk, France). Bual's raisin aromas and flavor are a great match for a softer, richer cheese with complexity. Try Serra da Estrela (sheep milk, Portugal), a springy cheese with notes of butter, nuts, and a touch of hay.

MATCH MADE IN HEAVEN

Zamorano (sheep milk, Spain) with Marcona almonds, a slice of membrillo, and a Bual Madeira. The cheese is nutty and salty with a little bit of complexity from aging. Marcona almonds are fried in sunflower oil until they are crispy, and then lightly salted. The membrillo is thick and sweet, adding a delightfully light note to match with the raisin notes of the wine and offset the saltiness of the cheese and nuts. This is a fantastic combination to enjoy at the end of an evening of Spanish or Portuguese tapas!

FACT

The islands of Madeira have a long history of winemaking dating back to the early fifteenth century, when Madeira was a popular port of call.

PORT

Made in the Douro region of Portugal, port is the most popular of all fortified wines. It was originally made as a table wine, but producers discovered that adding distilled spirits to the fermenting wine turned it into the sweet, smooth treat we enjoy today. Modern wine laws allow over a hundred different grape varietals to be used in making port!

THE WINE

The secret to port is the addition of grape spirits during the wine's fermentation. Essentially, fermentation is converting grape sugar into alcohol. When it is done to completion, the resulting wine is alcoholic but not sweet. When you add raw spirits to the mix, it halts the fermentation process immediately and any sugars left over stay sweet. For port, that means the wine has more alcohol, and still has some sugar left that wasn't converted, making the wine high octane and sweet! While White Port is somewhat available, port from red grapes is far more popular, and comes in two styles. Ruby Port is fortified red wine that is stored away from oxygen, allowing the wine to keep its ruby red color and bright red fruit aromas and color. Tawny Port is aged in oak barrels with constant exposure to oxygen. This contact turns the wine a tawny brown as it ages and imparts wonderfully nutty aromas and flavors of toffee, vanilla, and raisins. The longer Tawny Port ages (ten, twenty, or even thirty years), the more those characteristics are developed.

THE CHEESE THAT LOVES IT

Cheeses that are flavorful and medium hard work well with port. Ruby Port pairs beautifully with the classic Montgomery's Clothbound Cheddar (cow milk, England). The cheese's curdy texture and slightly sweet and farmy flavors blend seamlessly with the wine's fruit and thickness. Ruby Ports also work well with soft cheeses that have a slight saltiness to them. For Tawny Ports, cheeses with a nuttiness to them work well. Try an aged Reypenaer VSOP (cow milk, The Netherlands). The nutty, sweet flavors of the cheese match the wine's toffee character.

MATCH MADE IN HEAVEN

There can be only one. The classic English blue cheese Stilton (cow milk, England) with Tawny Port and some toasted hazelnuts. Or some raisins. Or dried figs. It almost doesn't matter. The world-class flavor combination of the earthy, silky cheese and sweet wine are spectacular all on their own. Adding the nuts or figs brings another complementary flavor to this all-star team.

SAUTERNES

This gorgeous wine hails from Bordeaux, France, and is considered some of the world's best white wine. Noble and magnificent, a well-made Sauternes has an aroma and flavor that continually excite and captivate wine lovers the world over.

THE WINE

Sauternes is made from Sauvignon Blanc, Sémillion, and Muscadelle grapes that have been affected by *Botrytis cinerea*, known as "noble rot," which concentrates the sugars in the grapes significantly. The result is a wine that is aromatic and heady, with an incredible array of aromas that include candied fruits, honeysuckle, pineapple, citrus, vanilla, ginger, heather . . . the list can go on and on. The more you pay attention to the aroma, the more the wine will reveal. The flavor is no less enticing, with rich sweetness balanced by bright acidity and flavors of white peach, nectarine, honey, pears, apples, and other light fruits. These wines can be simply majestic.

THE CHEESE THAT LOVES IT

Sauternes's depth of flavor and full body can handle big, strong cheeses. Washed-rind cheeses add a touch of funk that works well with Sauternes's white fruit notes. Try U Bel Fiuritu (sheep milk, France), a pungent, spicy cheese from Corsica that is rich and creamy, with a slight herbaceousness. Hard cheeses work well, as long as they have a bit of nuttiness or fruitiness to them for the wine to play with. Try the fantastic Pleasant Ridge Extra-Aged Reserve (cow milk, United States). This award-winning, alpine-style cheese is both fruity and nutty when young, and evolves to be more savory as it ages, a fantastic profile for this wine.

MATCH MADE IN HEAVEN

The equally regal blue cheese Roquefort (sheep milk, France). As Stilton is to port, Roquefort is to Sauternes—the perfect match. The cheese's minerality and slight saltiness are perfectly matched to the wine's deep fruit notes and viscous body. Though there is no need for a condiment that can improve this duo, those from southern France often enjoy this combination with rye bread studded with black currants. The bread's dark, deep notes act as a foil for the cheese and wine's brighter flavors. This is a perennial after-dinner favorite!

SHERRY

Made for centuries in the Spanish municipality of Jerez, sherry (locally known as Xerez) has long been considered one of Europe's finest wines. This versatile wine differs from port because the wine is fortified after it is fermented, not during fermentation, as port is. This means a drier, nuttier wine that is rarely sweet.

THE WINE

Sherry is made from three grape varietals: Palomino, Pedro Ximénez, and Moscatel. There are five main types. Fino is the lightest and palest, with aromas of sea air, pears, and almonds, and flavors that are fruity, nutty, and a little bit savory. Manzanilla is aged a bit longer. The aromas and flavors of olives, apples, and minerals lead you to flavors that are fruity with a delicious hint of chalkiness and brine. Amontillado is exposed to air for a while, darkening the wine a little from the oxidation. This wine is dry, with aromas and flavors of almonds, cedar wood, and dried fruits, and a hint of sea air and brine. Oloroso sherries are oxidized even longer, making them the darkest and most alcoholic of them all. Aromas of leather, cedar, dried fruits, sea air, and exotic spices are common. Oloroso sherries have flavors of macadamia nuts, dried apricots and figs, citrus peel, and brine. Cream is a general term used for artificially sweetened and colored sherries, usually Olorosos. They can be fun to sip, but don't have the same magnificence their cousins bring to the glass.

THE CHEESE THAT LOVES IT

Generally, the fruity and briny flavors of sherry go well with cheeses that have a little age and personality to them. For the drier, lighter fino, try Idiazabal (sheep milk, Spain). The cheese has a lovely smokiness that is cut by the wine. Manzanilla pairs well with cheeses that have a bit of saltiness to them. Amontillado's darker personality makes it a great partner for Cheddar's complex texture and flavors. Oloroso can handle longer aged cheeses with ease.

MATCH MADE IN HEAVEN

Fino sherry with Manchego Añejo (sheep milk, Spain), green olives, and a paper-thin slice or two of jamón. This classically Spanish combination is amazingly flavorful. The Manchego is assertive but smooth, with a dry texture, and finishes with a bite. The briny olives and salty charcuterie bring out the salinity and nuttiness of the wine. This is really a treat to experience.

VIN DOUX NATUREL

The Languedoc–Roussillon region of southwest France has been enjoying these lightly fortified wines since the fourteenth century, when the recipe was perfected. As with port, spirits are added to the fermentation to make it higher in alcohol and sweet. In this case, brandy is used. It is made in both white and red styles. The name itself translates to "natural sweet wine," a good sign for a dessert wine!

THE WINE

Vin doux naturels come in two styles. The red wines are made from the Grenache grape, and come from Banyuls and Maury (and will be labeled that way). They have aromas of candied orange peel, ginger, cinnamon, and caramel, and can be mildly spicy. The white wines are made from several different varieties of Muscat grapes, and all have a powerful fresh fruit aroma that can also include citrus and flowers. Flavors of peach, spices, exotic fruits, and dried fruits are common.

THE CHEESE THAT LOVES IT

Vin doux naturels are great wines to pair with cheese because the higher alcohol and bright fruit notes meld with stronger cheese flavors, especially those found in blue cheeses. Try a Banyuls with Stichelton (cow milk, England). This cheese is essentially a raw-milk Stilton recipe, and so it shares many of the same characteristics, but with more funk and depth. The sweet, red wine softens the edges of the pairing rather well!

MATCH MADE IN HEAVEN

White vin doux naturel with MitiBleu (sheep milk, Spain). This cheese is similar to French Roquefort. Sharp, bright tones of blue and balanced saltiness keep the flavor of the cheese clean. The wine's naturally fresh characteristics keep the pairing as light and refreshing as a combination of blue cheese and fortified wine can be! A daub of apricot preserves emphasizes the wine's fruitiness and sweetens the flavor of the cheese a bit.

FACT

Oxidation plays an important role in the decision-making of the winemaker. That intentional exposure to oxygen helps shape the color, aroma, and flavor of the final wines. More exposure will yielder a darker, nuttier wine while less exposure will let wines keep more of their grapey, fresh notes.

VIN SANTO

Vin Santo is made unlike almost any other wine in the world. The grapes are laid out on straw mats in warm rooms to allow them to dry over days. The resulting wine can be bone-dry all the way to extremely sweet depending on the winemaker. This Tuscan gem was originally used in holy rites and masses in the Renaissance era, earning it the moniker Vin Santo—"holy wine."

THE WINE

Made from Trebbiano and Malvasia grapes, Vin Santo is intense and flavorful, partly from the concentrated sugars from drying the grapes and also because the wine is aged in small wood barrels for several years. These wines have aromas of toffee and caramel, toasted nuts, earth, and honey. The flavor is equally rich, with a thick body and flavors of vanilla, candied citrus peel, and dried fig, with a slight nuttiness on the finish.

THE CHEESE THAT LOVES IT

Because Vin Santo is so sweet, it can be a little more difficult to pair with cheeses than other dessert wines. A little out-of-the-box thinking is called for here. Pair this wine with desserts featuring cheese. A well-made cheesecake would be a great choice, because the dessert is sweet enough to not get lost in the wine. Cannoli, with sweet ricotta cheese filling, is another delicious pairing option.

MATCH MADE IN HEAVEN

Whipped ricotta with a drizzle of citrus blossom honey and Vin Santo. The light and airy ricotta (made by blending fresh ricotta cheese, a little milk, and some honey together for a few seconds in a food processor) has just the right body to match the wine. The honey adds sweetness to the cheese, which matches the wine, and the light orange scent brings out the vanilla and oak notes in the aroma of the wine. This is a great dessert combination after a rich and satisfying meal.

FACT

This wine, and others like it, is sometimes referred to as a "straw wine," which refers to the process of drying grapes in the sun prior to pressing them. This drying intensifies the grape's flavors and significantly increases the sugar-to-juice ratio, yielding a sweeter wine. Originally, the grapes would be dried in clusters in the sun for several days. Now, value-focused winemakers can use artificial drying methods to accelerate the process.

(7)

CONDIMENTS

A plate. One (or several) wedges of tasty cheese. A glass of favorite wine, perhaps some bread. Is the plate complete? Are you ready to dig in? That depends. Do you want to add another flavor or texture? Condiments are a great way to add just the right note you're looking for. They can be as simple as a few walnuts or as complex as a fruit chutney. Sadly, most people haven't had luck with condiments, haven't thought to use them, or (worst of all) only ever use fig jam. It's time to broaden the horizons to see the nearly endless possibilities.

Of all the comments I've received during my years of teaching, one of the most frequent (and, frankly, most surprising) is students' surprise at how much they enjoyed the unexpected condiment served. Whether it's a dollop of lemon jam or a chunk of dark chocolate, condiments catch many people a bit off guard, and they are usually pleasantly surprised at the combination. Not everyone, of course. Purists tend to scoff at what they feel is a wholly unnecessary extra addition, and that's fine. There's plenty of room for different opinions, even if it means they miss out on the amazing explosion of flavor a bit of cherry jam brings to Manchego and a sip of Rioja.

THE BASICS OF CONDIMENTS

In broad terms, condiments can be categorized as either sweet or savory. Some teeter on both, however, which is okay. Using condiments is an inexact science, and is best enjoyed through lots of experimentation!

SWEET CONDIMENTS

This family mostly includes fruit and fruit-based foods. Jams, jellies, honeys, dried fruit, and the like are all part of this team. The strength of this family is the ability to add fruit flavor to the pairing, as well as fruit sugars, which can make the combination feel fuller when eaten. There are a few basic categories of sweet condiments.

Chocolate: Everyone's favorite food makes a great companion to wine and cheese as long as well-made chocolate is used. Cheap chocolate often incorporates paraffin (food wax) and palm or canola oil to bulk up the chocolate. These fillers make the cheese and wine taste waxy and unpleasant. No good. If you're going to use chocolate, splurge for the good stuff. Chocolate can add all sorts of character, depending on the cacao level of the chocolate being used. Milk chocolate (which has more sweeteners and milk than cacao) lends soft, milky notes and mild chocolate flavor, a great addition to a piece of Brie, for example. Dark chocolate (which has more cacao and very little sweetener or milk added) can bring complex notes of berries, coffee, vanilla, and lots of other flavors to the party. These more intense flavors pair fantastically with blue cheeses in particular, although a chunk of dark chocolate paired with an aged piece of Parmigiano-Reggiano is pretty awesome. It's all about matching intensities.

Dark chocolate is an excellent companion to rich and strong cheeses (especially blue cheese!).

Conserves: These are fruits cooked with nuts and chunks of dried fruit. They are extremely chunky and heavy. Mixing in the nuts and additional dried fruit adds a layer of complexity to the flavor and texture, and can be quite tasty. These are great with aged cheeses that may have a bit of nuttiness to them as well. The combination emphasizes those qualities, and creates a salty-sweet complement.

Fruit: Whether dried or fresh, fruit makes an excellent condiment for pairing because it directly adds a flavor and also contributes acidity, which adds brightness and freshness to the pairing. Dried fruit is a little mellower but is typically sweeter. Fresh fruit in season is extremely versatile and delicious. In either case, the fruit will usually team up more strongly with the wine because of the fruit flavor connection. Try to identify the fruit flavors in the wine and use that fruit to really make the flavor punch out.

Don't be that person who only ever serves fig jam. Be creative!

Honey's sweetness and texture meld with many soft and opulent cheeses.

Fruit Butters: Fruit butters are made from cooking fruit slowly for a long time, reducing the texture to that resembling butter. (There is no actual butter, or any dairy, in fruit butter. It's only named for the similar texture.) While fruit butters are undeniably delicious, they are usually not the best choice for pairing with cheese because they tend to not be strong enough to stand up to cheese. Fruit butters are at their best as fillings and spreads.

Honey: Honey can be a fantastic choice for a pairing. The sweetness and coating texture bring a smile to pretty much anyone. It's important to keep in mind that honey is an incredibly intense food. Even though it can be sweet, the aromas and mouthfeel are extremely powerful. (The next time you have a jar of honey, stick your nose right in there and take a deep whiff. You'll see what I mean.) Use honey in moderation when pairing. A little goes a long way.

It's also important to pick the right honey for the job. Acacia honey is light and floral, a great choice for soft cheeses and goat cheeses. Chestnut honey is deeper and richer, best served with fuller cheeses and those with aggressive aromas (the "stinky" washed-rind cheeses). And French or Italian *melata* (honey

made from tree sap instead of flower pollen) is dark and brooding, with a flavor that is a cross between molasses and fresh grape juice. This would be ideal with bold, strong blue cheeses.

Marmalades: These are made with citrus and incorporate the rind of the fruit in addition to the juice and pulp. The goal of a marmalade is to extract the bitter citrus oil that is just underneath the rind of the fruit. This is why you can't have a strawberry marmalade—strawberries don't have rinds, and therefore no bitter oil to extract. You can have strawberry *in* a marmalade, but there has to be a citrus fruit included to provide the oil. This condiment is all about the sweet-bitter combination, and works really well with fresh goat cheeses because the condiment is as tangy and forward as the cheese itself.

Jellies: These are made with gelatin and the juice of a fruit (or the flavoring of a fruit). They are usually a little bit see-through and quite sweet. The most common flavors include strawberry, grape, and other berry flavors. They are a good choice for cheeses with some body and age to them. A great example is Cheddar cheese with apple cider jelly. The sweet jelly keeps it simple and fruity with the thick texture of the cheese.

Preserves and Jams: These are made with the juice and the pulp of the fruit. For jam, the pulp is usually crushed. In preserves, the pulp is left more intact for a chunky texture. If the fruit has exterior seeds, they are usually left in (strawberries are the best example). These are fantastic with cheeses that have mild, rather than aggressive, flavors. A personal favorite is Comté with wild strawberry preserves.

SAVORY CONDIMENTS

These condiments are used because they add a "serious" note to the pairing instead of a sweet note. Many people prefer this kind of condiment because they don't have much of a sweet tooth, or they are serving a wine that has no sweetness and want to keep the pairing that way. Other people like using savory condiments because some add texture and depth to the combination. There are many different kinds of savory condiments, each with its own charm.

Nuts: Nuts are a great way to add texture and flavor to a pairing. It's important to keep in mind the characteristics of the nuts you're thinking of using. Unsalted, plain macadamia nuts are mild and subtle, a great partner for cheeses with a similarly mild disposition. Toasted hazelnuts have a distinct flavor, one that happens to pair almost seamlessly with oaked Chardonnays. Salted cashews are meaty and dense. Almonds have that distinct flavor. Walnuts are a little bit tannic. Each nut has its own strengths. Play to that.

Oils: These are a way to add flavor without adding too much texture or weight. The most common oil used is, of course, olive oil, but it doesn't stop there. Not by a long shot. Pistachio oil is gorgeous on aged pecorino cheeses. Roasted pumpkin seed oil adds a lovely note to semi-hard cheeses. For a

Oils from olives and nuts add complexity and flavor to cheeses without adding too much weight.

real treat, get a bottle of Italian agrumato—olive oil pressed with citrus peel to infuse the flavor. Lemon agrumato drizzled over fresh mozzarella is almost beyond words. There is a wide array of oils available now that add nuttiness or sweetness, fruity notes or smoky tones. Don't hesitate to explore and experiment.

Vegetables and Herbs: An onion is a vegetable. It's also the traditional accompaniment (with rye bread) to German Muenster cheese. Bell pepper aromas are often found in Cabernet Sauvignons. Basil is a classic addition to buffalo mozzarella. Vegetables can add crunch and juiciness or savory tones to pairings. These are a little harder to pair with cheeses and wines because not too many wines have vegetal aromas or flavors, making it more challenging to integrate them. In general, use milder cheeses with softer textures (like fontina, for example) with veggies that have snap and crispness to them (like celery, bell peppers, or carrots). Above all, have an open mind with these. Really interesting combinations can be had!

Vinegar: Vinegar is all about acid, and that is important to remember when pairing with cheese. It can be done, but not all vinegars will go with all cheeses. Keep in mind how strong the vinegar is, and pick a cheese that offsets the acidity. The easiest vinegar to use is balsamic vinegar because extended aging has thickened and sweetened the vinegar, making it a great combination with salty, aged cheeses (most notably, Parmigiano-Reggiano). White wine vinegar with vanilla is flavorful and not too heavy. Vinegars can also be used by reducing them in a saucepan over low heat until they thicken, turning them into more of a sauce. They also work well with cooked cheeses. The Sicilian antipasto *caciu all'Argintera* calls for young pecorino cheese to be baked and then sprinkled with red wine vinegar and dried herbs. Then it's baked a little while longer to let the flavors meld together. The tangy vinegar contrasts with the melted cheese.

SOME CLASSIC COMBINATIONS

The world has been enjoying wine and cheese for a long time, both separately and together. Over time, particular combinations have come together that simply rise above the others. They are the perfect synthesis of taste and texture, flavor and culture. Here are a few of the best.

Buffalo Mozzarella with Olive Oil and Fresh Basil with Orvieto: This may be the greatest summer combination I know of. The delicately milky flavor of the cheese marries perfectly with the aromatic basil. The rich, supple texture of the cheese complements the viscosity of the olive oil. The wine is fresh and lively. The whole combination is sunny and bright. Amazing.

Camembert, Apples, and Chardonnay: The northwest French region of Normandy is as well known for these little wheels of bloomy-rinded cheese as they are for their apples. Naturally, they pair together beautifully. The apple's natural acidity cuts through the richness of the cheese, and adds a bright, crisp flavor. Most Chardonnays have an apple note to them, emphasizing the fruit. Try this with an oaked Chardonnay—the creamy body and the sweet vanilla and wood tones of the wine become the central meeting place for the cheese and apples.

Langres, Acacia Honey, and Champagne: Langres, a cow milk cheese from Champagne, France, is such a perfect partner to the sparkler that the makers even leave an indentation on the top (called a fontaine) for Champagne to be poured into! The firm and supple interior almost melts in the mouth, leaving a complex flavor. The honey sweetens the cheese slightly and thickens the impression in your mouth—perfect for the bubbles to come in and rinse away in anticipation for the next sip! The wine's bready, yeasty aroma melds so nicely with the cheese and honey. An opulent combination.

Manchego, Membrillo, and Rioja: Sheep milk cheese is big and flavorful, and Manchego is the perfect example of that. Sharp, full flavors command attention. Any condiment used needs to be as prominent, and the sweet and thick quince paste called membrillo is more than up for the task. It is a beautifully flavorful accompaniment that sates the Spanish love of sweet and salty. Rioja, the classic Spanish red wine, is full-bodied and smooth. Oaking has given the wine complexity and warm tones, bringing together the salty cheese and the sweet paste almost effortlessly. A magnificent trio.

Parmigiano-Reggiano, Aged Balsamic Vinegar, and Chianti Classico: The king of all cheeses meets its match in flavorful intensity in balsamic vinegar. The sweet-and-sour profile of the vinegar is right at home with the salty cheese. The wine is all cherry and wood notes, adding equally intense flavors to the combination. The wine's tannins soak up the salt and sweet of the others, blending together into a full, rich mouthful.

Roquefort, Black Currant Bread, and Sauternes: This is one of the great classic combinations in the culinary world. Both the wine and the cheese come from the southwestern part of France. Roquefort, considered one of the three kings of blue cheese (with England's Stilton and Italy's Gorgonzola), is bold and sharp with minerally precision and an addictive salty balance that is as perfect as it gets. The wine is honeyed and thick, with heady aromas of apricots and flowers, the perfect counterpart to the cheese's edges. In that neck of the woods, this pairing is classically enjoyed simply with currant bread or raisin bread. Try this regal combination at least once!

Stilton, Dried Figs, and Tawny Port: Another world-class combination. The cheese is noble and layered, with a creamy and silky texture and a farmy flavor that is at once sweet, milky, and blued. The figs add a heavy sweet note, which is a top-notch lead-in to the wine's similarly sweet notes of vanilla, toffee, and . . . figs! A glorious combination that appears on many, many holiday dinner tables (including mine!).

Valençay Frais, Lemon Preserves, and Sauvignon Blanc: This tangy, zippy combination comes from the Loire Valley in France. The cheese, a fresh goat cheese, is striking to look at—an ash-covered pyramid, with bright lactic flavors and a finish that is citrusy and gently sour. The preserves carry the lemon flavor while adding sugary richness to the cakey cheese. The Sauvignon Blanc grape is thought to have originated in the Loire, and so it is right at home with notes of citrus and white fruits, tying it all together in a crisp, refreshing package.

A FINAL THOUGHT

Few pairing topics are more polarizing than whether or not to use condiments. As I mentioned, many purists eschew them. Many adventurous eaters love them. Most people are more surprised by them than anything. Personally, I think they add dimension and character to wine and cheese pairings. They make the experience all the more interesting, more intriguing. More enjoyable. In the end, isn't that the whole point?

TIPS AND TRICKS

HOW TO STORE WINE

When it comes to storing wine, remember that the vast majority of wines you might purchase are meant to be enjoyed within a few years of the release date, and aren't really suitable for extensive aging. If you want to get in to aging wines, fantastic! However, you should consider a much more formal and professional system. Otherwise, there are a few basics to keep in mind that will help get the most from your wines.

Temperature. Heat is an enemy of wine. When storing wine, environments that sustain or exceed 70°F/21°C will accelerate the aging of your wine, making it taste dull and flat. Ideally, wine should be stored around 55° F/13°C (the average temperature of a home cellar, for example). Don't worry if you can't arrange that. It can be warmer (up to 65°F/18°C) without any harm to wines that you're planning to drink sooner rather than later. On the other end of the tolerance scale is cold. Temperatures below 45°F/7°C can damage wine as well. That's the reason storing wine in your fridge isn't a great idea. Most home fridges chill below 45°F/7°C to safely refrigerate foods. Wines kept at this temperature for too long run the risk of having their corks constrict and dry out, allowing air into the bottle. The change in air pressure may even push the cork out of the bottle a little! Also, don't store wine in the unheated garage in the winter. Such low temperatures can freeze the wine, which may make it expand, causing the bottle to explode.

Light. Even though heat is wine's main enemy, it's not the only one. Light can also do bad things to wine, particularly sunlight. The sun's UV rays wreak havoc on the wine, prematurely aging it. Keep wines out of sunlight whenever possible when storing them. Household lights won't cause any real damage beyond making the wine labels fade over an extended period of time, which is only really a factor if you plan on aging your bottles.

Positioning. Natural cork is porous, which is beneficial for wine because it lets in microscopic amounts of air. This "micro oxygenation" allows the wine to gracefully age over time if done correctly. However, cork is also subject to drying out. An overly dry cork will constrict, letting in too much air (even though it's a tiny amount). Fortunately, there's an easy fix: lay the bottles down to keep wine in contact with the cork. Problem solved!

Vibrations: Wine is happiest when it is still. Shaking bottles agitates the wine, which may accelerate the chemical reactions occurring in the bottle. If the wine is a sparkling wine, pressure builds up in the bottle, making it more dangerous when opened. Keep bottles still as much as possible.

In a nutshell, keep your wines in a cool, dry place where they can peacefully rest on their sides and wait until it's their time to shine! If you're drinking your wines as fast as you're buying them, a simple rack out of the sunlight works great. If you find yourself diving a little bit deeper, a rack in the basement or a wine cooler may be a better option to keep your bottles in tip-top shape.

IDEAL WINE SERVING TEMPERATURES AND THE 15-MINUTE RULE

Serving wine seems pretty straightforward, right? Open the bottle, maybe let it breathe a little bit, and then pour. What could be simpler? Although this series of steps is easy to follow, many people overlook one of the most important aspects to serving wine—the temperature. Serving wine at the correct temperature is an easy way to make sure you're getting the most enjoyment out of each sip.

People think it's best to drink white wines cold and red wines at room temperature. Unfortunately, that usually results in white wines being served at refrigerator temperature (too cold) and red wines being served at the temperature of the wine rack in the living room from which the bottle came (too warm). In both cases, the wines aren't at their best because of the temperature.

The best wine temperature for wine depends on what kind of wine it is. Sparkling wines are best when they are chilled and the bubbles are lively, around 48°F to 50°F/9°C to 10°C. Because of the refreshment factor is so important to rosé wines, they like to be chilled as well, around 50°F to 52°F/10°C to 11°C. White wines like to be just a hint warmer, around 53°F to 55°F/12°C to 13°C to allow the more complex and interesting aromas to emerge. Red wines are happy in the 62°F to 65°F/17°C to 18°C range, which is cellar temperature in most people's houses.

These are ideal ranges, of course. Wines don't have to be served precisely at these temperatures to be enjoyable. If you can't manage your refrigeration to such an exacting extent, don't worry too much about it. There's a quick and easy guideline many wine nerds follow—the 15-minute rule. If you're serving a white wine, take it out of the fridge 15 minutes before you're going to drink it. That gives the wine just enough time to warm up a touch and release its aromas. If you're drinking a red wine that's been in your parlor or a similarly warm room, put the bottle in the fridge for 15 minutes. It certainly isn't enough time to chill the wine, but it will take the edge off the temperature just a bit, making the wine a little more refreshing and focused.

DECANTING: LETTING THE WINE CATCH ITS BREATH

Decanting is a great way to not only make older wines shine their brightest, but also to give younger wines a chance to stretch their legs a bit and show what they've got.

Decanting is essentially mixing air with wine and then letting it sit still for a bit. It serves two purposes. For older wines, it lets the sediment sink to the bottom of the decanter so it doesn't add any astringency or bitterness to the flavor. For younger wines, it lets air gently blend in and release the aromas and flavors that make them so enjoyable.

It's easy to do, too. For younger wines, simply pour the wine into a decanter and let it sit for 15 to 30 minutes (the heavier the wine, the longer the time is best). For older wines, pour the wine into a decanter slowly to keep as much sediment in the bottle as possible. Once in the vessel, let it breathe for 30 to 60 minutes. That's it!

There are, of course, exceptions to the rule. If you're decanting a huge red wine such as Barolo or Bordeaux, longer decanting times are better. There are older versions that love to be decanted 4, 5, or even 6 hours! In those cases, a quick online search or chat with your wine shop pro will provide the ideal decanting time.

WHICH IS BETTER FOR WINE—CORKS OR SCREW CAPS?

Traditional corks are better for wine than screw caps. Unless they aren't. But they are, right? Sometimes. Confused yet? You're not alone. Screw caps have been gaining significant ground in the wine sealing game for the past thirty years, but they are still as misunderstood as they were when they first came out.

The mission of screw caps (known professionally as Stelvin closures) is clear: to keep wine in better condition for a longer time by preventing unwanted excess oxygen from seeping into the bottle through micro-porous corks. When they first hit the wine market back in the 1950s, almost everyone associated with wine loved the idea. Winemakers loved the cap because it kept their product in tip-top condition. Retailers no longer worried about rotted or dried corks ruining inventory, costing them money. Restaurants loved it because now any waiter could properly open a bottle of wine with just a flick of the wrist.

The only group that didn't welcome the Stelvin closure with open arms was unfortunately the most important—consumers. They viewed the screw cap as cheap, especially when serving wine from the bottle. Many discerning wine drinkers envisioned an intimate, candlelight dinner. The wine is presented. The chemistry of the moment builds more and more until . . . skrick! The bottle opens with all the ceremony of a soda.

Admittedly, there is no romance to Stelvin closure wines. However, it's been shown that wines benefit from the total seal the screw cap provides. They stay fresher longer, and drastically reduce incidents of spoiled wines. Fortunately, more and more winemakers are coming around to the cost and preservation benefits of these caps. It seems the public is becoming more comfortable with them as well—almost 90 percent of all wines coming from New Zealand and Australia employ the Stelvin closure. The more prominent wine regions are changing their minds as well. Spain, Italy, and even (gulp) France offer many screw cap wines.

HOW LONG WILL MY OPEN BOTTLE OF WINE LIVE?

This is another frequently asked question. The super-helpful answer is, of course, it depends.

When you open a bottle of wine, oxygen is allowed into the bottle, mixing with the wine. This oxidation is what causes wine to deteriorate. Unfortunately, once that clock has started ticking, it can't be stopped. High-tech bottle sealers, the little hand pumps that can be used, even cans of exotic gases to "seal" the bottle are only capable of slowing the effects of oxygen. An opened bottle of wine has somewhere between one and three days before it's no longer the wine you enjoyed when you first opened it.

The good news is some wines fare better than others. Though oxygen is the enemy, wine's acidity, sugar levels, and tannins help to preserve it. The more of them in the wine, the longer the lifespan. So, that bottle of Riesling that has high acidity and sugar? It will live longer than the Sauvignon Blanc you opened over the weekend. Other factors are in play as well. Older wines tend to deteriorate more quickly than younger ones. Wines that are vacuum-sealed after being opened will live longer than wines that aren't. Refrigerated wines live longer because the colder temperature slows down the effect of oxidation. Even the amount of wine left in the bottle matters. The more wine in the bottle, the less oxygen can get in. A bottle two-thirds full will live a little bit longer than a bottle that is almost empty.

Basically, if you vacuum-seal your wine and keep it in the fridge, you have approximately a day or two to enjoy it at its best. Ultimately, though, all that matters is you enjoy drinking it, even if it's day five! Let your taste buds be the judge.

ARE CHEESE RINDS EDIBLE?

To eat or not to eat the rind? That is frequently the question. When it comes to cheese rinds, you can eat it if you can eat it. (Helpful, right?) What I mean is this: If the rind is synthetic, don't consume it. If the cheese is covered in cloth (like some Cheddars), don't eat the cloth. If it's covered in wax (like many Goudas), don't eat the wax. Synthetic rinds are generally not edible.

Otherwise, the rinds are naturally occurring and edible. Be warned, though. Just because they are edible does not mean they will taste good. The rind on a wheel of Parmigiano-Reggiano, for example, is completely natural and therefore edible. Bite into a piece, however, and you're in for a lot of chewing on a rough, oily, thick chunk of rind that is nowhere near the edible delight the interior of the cheese is! It is much tastier when flavoring some broth with tortellini and spinach. Brie is a great example of a rind that is well worth eating. It is soft and almost chewy, with a flavor and texture different (yet complementary) to the cheese inside. Camembert? The rind is totally edible. Aged Gruyere? Edible but not all that tasty. Vacuum-sealed goat log from the supermarket. Nope, plastic's not edible.

Rinds play an important role in a wheel of cheese's development. Don't hesitate to try even a tiny nibble of natural rinds you come across, and toss the manmade ones.

BUYING AND STORING CHEESE

When buying cheese, find a source you can trust and that is reliable, not only for food safety reasons, but also to be certain you're getting authentic cheeses from someone who knows them and can answer any questions you may have. (No buying cheese from the van down by the river, no matter how much cheaper they may be.) There are many specialty retailers, farmer's markets, and cheese shops available to be of assistance. There are even several online retailers who provide excellent products at reasonable prices.

Check the dates on sealed pieces to ensure they are in the best possible condition before buying. For cheeses being cut off of wheels to your order, check the slice to make sure it's in good condition and looks great. Cheeses that are approaching the end of their lifespan should be avoided. They've already begun to deteriorate a bit, and won't give you the best flavor and texture. Whenever possible, taste the cheese you're considering. Most reputable shops will be happy to provide a small sample. It's important to taste the cheese because each wheel of cheese will be slightly different—part of the magic of real cheese! Trying a little taste is the best way to make sure you'll be happy with your choice.

Buy only as much cheese as you need in the short-term (up to a week), not a large quantity to hold you over for a long period of time. For example, it's fine to buy a bit of Parmigiano-Reggiano to have in the fridge for the week, or a few cheeses on a Thursday for a Saturday night dinner party. Just try to avoid buying a huge chunk to last the next month. When cheese is cut from a wheel, it immediately begins to slowly dry out. If you take too long to enjoy that piece, it will be past its peak condition, and you're no longer getting what you paid for!

Storing cheese is pretty easy. Keep uneaten cheese wrapped in breathable cheese paper whenever possible (usually stores are accommodating if you ask for a couple extra sheets when you're there). If cheese paper isn't available, wax paper, parchment paper, and even tin foil will work. Do NOT use plastic wrap, sealable plastic bags, or anything like that. Remember, cheese is a living, breathing organism with enzymes and bacteria hard at work. Sealing them off in plastic suffocates their air supply, and that's not good! Store your cheese in the veggie drawer of your fridge because the cooler temperature (around 40°F/4°C) and slightly higher humidity is beneficial to the cheese. Because the wrapping is permeable, don't store the cheese near any strong-flavored foods (for example, that piece of salmon you might have), because the cheese may pick up some of that food's aromas.

Last, if cheese in your fridge starts to get a little slimy or develop ammoniated aromas, toss it. It's a sign the cheese is well past its prime, and isn't in good condition to eat.

CAN YOU FREEZE CHEESE?

Generally, freezing cheese isn't a good idea. The extremely low temperature required for freezing can damage the structure of the cheese, resulting in a change in the texture of the cheese. Additionally, freezing alters the flavor of the cheese, usually for the worse. (Have you ever frozen chowder? When it's reheated, the potatoes are never the same. They become mealy and fall apart. Same idea with cheese.)

If you have already frozen cheese, or you like living dangerously, take care when you're thawing the cheese to eat (it pains me to even write that sentence). Place the cheese in the refrigerator for several hours to allow it to gently come back up to temperature. Once it's thawed, it will likely be drier and more crumbly from the exposure to extreme cold. It's best used in cooking at that point, rather than eating it on a cheese plate or straight-up.

WHAT'S THE STINKY IN STINKY CHEESES? (OR, DON'T FEAR THE SMELL.)

For many people, stinky cheeses are a total turnoff, and it's pretty much always because of the smell. As a cheese professional (and lover), it's sad to hear. These are some of the softest, creamiest, smoothest cheeses made, and the source of that smell is what is making it happen.

Washed-rind cheeses are cheeses that have some kind of moisture applied to the rind as it develops. Brine is the most common moisture used, but there are a wide range of options. Wine, beer, honey, and mead are just a few. As the wheel ages, the chosen liquid is lightly "washed" on to the rind. This additional moisture creates an inviting environment for a particular family of bacteria and yeasts to alight on the wheel and get to work. This typically turns the rind an orangey color, a trait shared by pretty much all washed-rind cheeses. As the bacteria works, outgassing occurs, creating that smell. It doesn't mean the cheese is bad. If you can brave the aroma, you'll be rewarded with a taste of cheese that is creamy and soft and salty on the inside— the result of the bacteria's hard work.

Here's a fun fact. Ever notice some cheeses smell a little bit like, well, feet? Why is that? The family of bacteria that work their magic on a wheel of washed-rind cheese, Brevibacterium linens, contains the same bacteria that make your feet smell. Now, don't panic. There aren't feet involved in the making of cheese. It's simply that the bacteria are related. Think of it in another way: Have you ever noticed that basil, spearmint, and oregano smell similar? Same idea. They're all from the same mint family, and so they share some common aromas even though they are different from one another.

Bottom line? Washed-rind cheeses may smell aggressive, but they are almost always soft, supple, and delicious on the inside. Don't fear the smell!

HOW DO I BUILD A ROCK STAR CHEESE PLATE?

People are sometimes a little hesitant to build a cheese plate. It's one thing to buy two or three cheeses you like and put them out for a party, and quite another to intentionally try and arrange and serve them in a progression. Fortunately, building a rock star cheese plate isn't as hard as it might seem. Although this topic could easily fill a book of its own, here are a few broad-stroke tips to consider.

Keep the list of cheeses short. When creating a cheese plate, consider its purpose. If it's the main attraction of the party or serving table, it's fine to offer up to five or so different cheeses. That gives you enough latitude to serve different textures and flavors without inundating your guests. If the cheese plate is being served at the end of a meal instead of a dessert, however, offer no more than three types of cheese. Anymore, and your guests may get a bit overwhelmed.

Vary the milks and textures. For an overall sampler, mix the milk types. For example, the cheese plate might include one goat milk cheese, one cow milk, and one sheep milk. The exception to this might be, for example, an all-goat milk sampler in the spring when goat milk cheeses are at their best. Then, of course, all goat milk cheeses would be appropriate. Try to mix up the textures as well to keep it interesting. A firm pecorino next to a gooey Taleggio and a cakey goat milk Selles sur Cher is a great example of variety in texture.

Consider your condiments. Pairing cheeses and condiments such as honey, nuts, mustards, and fruits, are a great way to add dimension and interest to your cheeses. Be careful not to overdo it, though. If you have three cheeses on your plate, don't serve five different condiments. Either pair each with a unique condiment, or serve one or two condiments suitable for pairing with all the cheeses, and let the consumer decide. There are some condiments that work well over a broad range of cheeses. Honey (especially acacia), toasted hazelnuts or walnuts, and figs (dry or fresh) are great all-purpose condiments that can give you lots of mileage on your cheese plate.

As with all pairings, the ultimate decider should be your palate, and what you're trying to achieve with your cheese plate. Have fun with it, and don't be afraid to try unusual pairings (think caramel, or Dijon mustard, or prunes)—you never know what you'll like!

ABOUT THE AUTHOR

Adam Centamore is a professional educator who conducts private and corporate cheese- and wine-tasting experiences with the goal of sharing the pure enjoyment of these foods. He is certified by the Elizabeth Bishop Wine Program, and is a member of the French Wine Society and Society of Wine Educators. He is also the Maître d'Fromage for the Boston chapter of the Chevaliers du Tastevin, a prestigious French wine society. By day, Adam works at Bin Ends, an award-winning wine retailer. He worked at and teaches at Formaggio Kitchen, a world-renowned cheese importer featuring artisanal cheeses, charcuterie, and condiments from Europe and the United States. Adam enjoys eating, drinking, and teaching about wine and cheese!

ACKNOWLEDGMENTS

I want to thank the many people who helped bring this book into being.

Thank you to Quarry Books for this amazing opportunity. I cannot express my gratitude and appreciation enough. I truly hope the final work justifies their investment in me. Thank you to my editor, Jonathan Simcosky, for his guidance and suggestions, and most importantly for having an open mind in the first place. Thank you to Marissa Giambrone and Glenn Scott for bringing my words to life visually. Their skills and talents were most welcome and appreciated. Also, thank you to Alisa Neely for her styling expertise.

Thank you to John Hafferty and the team at Bin Ends Wines for the use of their fantastic wines.

Thank you to Tim, Valerie, Ihsan, and everyone at Formaggio Kitchen for allowing me to develop and nurture my interest and passion for cheese and fine foods in general.

A special thank you to Diran Apelian for generously agreeing to write the foreword, and more importantly, for encouraging me to pursue this project. He taught me it all starts with a table of contents. I am grateful for his friendship and wisdom.

Thank you to my mom, Pam, for instilling in me a love of food and cooking from a young age, and my dad, Russ, for teaching me that work ethic and integrity are everything. Thank you to my sister Kendall and my brother Jesse, for their support, encouragement, and acceptance that I was always the favorite.

Last but absolutely not least, thank you to my beautiful wife Carmen and my amazing boys Massimo and Rudie. They bore the brunt of my many nights writing and time away from them to complete this project. It simply could not have come to fruition without their encouragement and support. I hope all the nights of eating cheese and drinking wine made up for at least some of it. I love you guys.

INDEX